The Bravewell Story

How a Small
Community of Philanthropists
Made a Big Difference in Healthcare

BONNIE J. HORRIGAN

FOREWORD BY HARVEY FINEBERG, MD, PhD

ACADEMIC CONSORTIUM FOR INTEGRATIVE MEDICINE & HEALTH

MCLEAN, VIRGINIA

The Academic Consortium for Integrative Medicine & Health would like to acknowledge The Bravewell Collaborative for providing generous support for the publication of this book.

For additional information please contact:
Academic Consortium for Integrative Medicine & Health
6728 Old McLean Village Drive
McLean, VA 22101
(703) 556-9222
www.imconsortium.org

Cover and interior design: Anne C. Kerns, Anne Likes Red, Inc.
Back cover photograph: xeipe/iStock/Thinkstock

First Printing, March 2016

ISBN 978-0-9888753-0-2

Printed in Cheverly, Maryland, USA

"If you want to go fast, go alone.
If you want to go far, go together."

— **African Proverb**

This book is dedicated to all
past, present, and future pioneers.
May you one day experience your vision
as a lived reality.

iv

CONTENTS

FOREWORD

I N AN ELECTRONICALLY CONNECTED WORLD, social media hold sway. Hundreds of millions of persons all over the globe connect with one another every day over the internet. The social media build unexpected coalitions, track and even foment revolutions, and create novel opportunities to find common ground with friends near and far.

At a time when we are increasingly tied to the electronic web, how refreshing it is to learn about a modern movement crafted the old-fashioned way, person-to-person, serendipitously and intentionally. The founding mothers and fathers of The Bravewell Collaborative shared a passion borne of personal experience—to make healthcare more responsive to the complete needs and well-being of the patient. From the outset, the lay champions of what came to be known as *integrative medicine* sought alliance with like-minded leaders in medicine, nursing, and other health professions. Together, they showed how the full range of physical and emotional needs of patients could be met by a combination of orthodox and complementary modalities of care. They fostered the application of integrative medicine concepts across the array of medical specialties, and especially in the care of patients with cancer. They changed the way many patients receive care today.

Along the way, Bravewell devised a distinctive form of strategic philanthropy: cooperative, focused, savvy, selective, and effective. They built institutions, nurtured a medical movement, educated professionals and laypersons, and showed how money well spent can benefit society. It took many hands and hearts to create the collaborative, and strong, selfless leadership made all the difference. Throughout its existence, Bravewell never lost sight of the patient at the center of all it strived to accomplish.

The test of Bravewell will be the durability of its message: Will medicine continue to progress along integrative lines focused on the whole patient, or will hyper-specialization lead to isolated treatment of a molecule or an organ? Will we focus only on a list of medical problems, or will we seek to understand the life goals of the patient and help to achieve them? If we want the concepts and practice of patient-centered care and integrative medicine to hold sway, then we can take heart from the model and achievement of The Bravewell Collaborative.

The history of The Bravewell Collaborative is a story of friendship, passion, vision, ingenuity, leadership, generosity, and commitment. It is a story of institution building and cultural transformation. It is a story of reshaping modern medicine. It is, ultimately, an entirely human story about the care and well-being of every one of us. It is a story worth savoring.

HARVEY V. FINEBERG, MD, PhD
President, Gordon and Betty Moore Foundation
Former President, Institute of Medicine
(now, National Academy of Medicine)

CHAPTER ONE

Self-Organization and Critical Connections

❧

"Never doubt that a small group of thoughtful,
committed citizens can change the world.
Indeed, it is the only thing that ever has."

— MARGARET MEAD

E VERY ONCE IN A WHILE, the right people come together at the right time to do the right thing and the world shifts. This book is about one of those times. It is about The Bravewell Collaborative, a group of people who saw the need for change, found each other, and then took collective action, helping to turn a small wave into a tidal surge of great consequence.

History has shown that this is what often occurs when one starts with good intent, combines forces with like minds, and stays the course, which is what The Bravewell Collaborative did during the fourteen years of its existence.

HOW CULTURES CHANGE

Commenting on the ways in which cultural change actually comes about, social and organizational scientist Margaret Wheatley advises that, "The world doesn't change one person at a time. It changes as networks of relationships form among people who discover they share a common cause and vision of what's possible."

For those who wish to make a difference in the world, her advice is to stop worrying about achieving critical mass and, instead, focus on fostering critical connections. "We don't need to convince large numbers of people to change; instead, we need to connect with kindred spirits," Wheatley explains. "Through these relationships, we will develop the new knowledge, practices, courage, and commitment that lead to broad-based change."

This observation certainly proved true in the case of The Bravewell Collaborative. Reflecting back, it is clear that *self-organization* was the organic process through which Bravewell came into existence and that developing *connections with kindred spirits* played an important role in how its members helped evolve the field of integrative healthcare. Further, the strategic initiatives Bravewell chose have, in fact, generated *new knowledge and practices*, and as the nexus of influence widened, as more people found *inspiration and community*, Bravewell's efforts bolstered the larger integrative healthcare community's *courage and commitment* to keep pushing forward.

Wheatley calls this phenomenon "emergence." She says, "Emergence is the process by which all large-scale change happens on this planet. Separate, local efforts connect and strengthen their interactions and interdependencies. What emerges as these become stronger is a *system of influence*, a powerful cultural shift that then greatly influences behaviors and defines accepted practices."

THE NEED FOR CHANGE

In the last decades of the twentieth century, people from many walks of life began to recognize that the American healthcare system was broken and unsustainable. Critics complained that the system was too fragmented into specialties and that its approach over-emphasized both technology and pharmaceuticals, at the expense of person-centered and holistic care. Despite all the scientific advances in health and medicine, the general population was increasingly unfit and burdened with chronic disease. Overall life expectancy was declining, healthcare costs were escalating out of control, patients were disgruntled, and provider burnout was becoming increasingly common.

But not everyone kept conducting business as usual. A few visionaries found new approaches that would improve care, even if only within their own institutions. As these pioneers took up this mantle of change, a new vision for healthcare began to emerge.

In 1979, Jon Kabat-Zinn, PhD, founded the Center for Mindfulness in Medicine, Health Care and Society at the University of Massachusetts Medical School in Worcester, Massachusetts. Through the Center, he began teaching a mindfulness meditation practice focused on helping people cultivate a greater awareness of the unity of their mind and body and the ways in which unconscious thoughts, feelings, and behaviors could affect emotional, physical, and spiritual health.

In 1984, Dean Ornish, MD, founded the Preventive Medicine Institute in Sausalito, California, in order to conduct scientific research concerning the effects of diet and lifestyle choices on health and disease. In 1990, he published the landmark Lifestyle Heart Trial in *The Lancet*, the first study to demonstrate that comprehensive lifestyle changes alone—quitting smoking, changing what we eat, improving how we respond to stress, increasing how much we exercise, and paying attention to the quality of our relationships— could reverse coronary artery disease.

Also in 1990, wishing to return love and compassion and the art of healing to medicine, Rachel Remen, MD, founded the Institute for the Study of Heath & Illness at Commonweal in Bolinas, California. Dr. Remen would later develop The Healer's Art, a course designed to reintegrate the heart and soul into medicine, which is now taught in more than half of the medical schools in the United States.

In October 1991, guided by Senator Tom Harkin, Congress enacted legislation that created the Office of Alternative Medicine at the National Institutes of Health and provided it with $2 million of funding so the value of healing practices from other cultures could be researched. That same year, Larry Dossey, MD, published *Meaning & Medicine*, which examined the mind-body connection and built on his earlier work, *Recovering The Soul*, and James Gordon, MD, founded the Center for Mind-Body Medicine in Washington, DC.

In 1993, with funding support from the Fetzer Institute and the Nathan Cummings Foundation among others, Bill and Judith Moyers produced the PBS Series *Healing and the Mind*, which examined the meaning of sickness and health and the undeniable connection between mind and body. Also in 1993, David Eisenberg, MD, published his groundbreaking survey in the *New England Journal of Medicine*, which revealed that 34 percent of American adults had used at least one unconventional therapy.

In 1994, Andrew (Andy) Weil, MD, established the Arizona Center for Integrative Medicine at the University of Arizona in Tucson, Arizona, with the goal of educating and actively supporting a new community of physicians who would embody the philosophy and practice of a healing-oriented medicine that focused on natural interventions, such as dietary changes and botanical supplements, and addressed the whole person—body, mind, and spirit.

However, despite the work of these and other visionaries, as well as the health benefits they could each demonstrate, the overall cultural climate within healthcare was less than friendly toward this new perspective on health and healing. In the 1980s and '90s, physicians wishing to study integrative approaches to care within the academic arena were often told that it was a career killer; conventional medical journals refused to publish manuscripts covering topics such as acupuncture or mind-body medicine; researchers found it hard to secure grants to investigate the efficacy of integrative approaches; and providers across the country were discouraged—and sometimes even banned—from including in their practice medical interventions from any other culture as well as what were then non-mainstream approaches such as nutritional supplementation and mind-body practices. Broad-scale adoption of the new approach to health and healthcare seemed to be an almost unattainable goal.

AN IDEA EMERGES

It was amid this backdrop that, in early 1996, Minneapolis resident Penny George received a devastating diagnosis—she had invasive breast cancer. The daughter of a physician and the wife of Bill George, then-CEO of Medtronic, Penny underwent a mastectomy followed by chemotherapy. In the process of her treatment, two things became obvious to her. "I knew that the physical aspects of the disease weren't the whole picture, and I knew that I had to take responsibility for getting myself out of the situation I was in. No one else could do it for me," she explains.

Penny determined that she needed to live in a new way and that she would start creating more health in everything she did. "I understood that I had to do everything I could to prevent the cancer from coming back," she adds. "And if I wasn't successful, if I was going to die from the cancer anyway, then I wanted to live the fullest life I could in the time I had left."

During that period of time, conventional healthcare could not help her achieve either of those goals; little attention was given to preventing cancer or to survivorship. The relationship between the physician and the patient was patriarchal, focusing solely on the disease and interventions such as surgery, radiation therapy, and chemotherapy—not on the individual as a whole human being.

Penny began to experiment on her own, going outside the mainstream to investigate different healing modalities including energy medicine, guided imagery, hypnotherapy, massage therapy, acupuncture, and even *pancha karma*, an Ayurvedic detoxification approach. Key to her healing process was that she loved the journey. "It wasn't so much about the things I did," she explains, "it was the fact that I was doing something to help myself and was creating my own healing team." She was also in psychoanalysis, which she says, "was a rope I held onto as I descended into the profound questions around death and the meaning of my life."

When she was on the road to health again, Penny—who had completed her doctorate in psychology just six months before her diagnosis and was a member of the Plymouth Congregational Church in Minneapolis, Minnesota—took a huge cultural and personal risk by going on an eleven-day vision quest in the Four Corners area of Utah. During four of those days, she was alone in the desert with only water to sustain her. "It was a profound and life-changing experience," she explains.

Penny came away from the vision quest more passionate about changing medicine than continuing to practice psychology. As a consequence, she and her husband Bill agreed that she would start taking the lead with the George Family Foundation, and focus primarily on integrative medicine. (For a definition of integrative medicine, see Chapter Five.)

A few months later, she was sitting on the front porch of her Minneapolis home with Diane Neimann, founder of Family Philanthropy Advisors (FPA) and an expert in family philanthropy and strategic planning. As they looked out at the serene Lake of the Isles, Diane asked Penny: "If you could change anything about the world, what would it be?"

Penny's answer was that she would *change the way medicine is practiced.*

MAKING PLANS

The George Family Foundation had hired FPA in 1998 to administer its giving, with Diane serving as the Foundation's executive director, so both Penny and Diane were aware of the fledgling movement to humanize medicine that was beginning to emerge in isolated pockets across the nation.

The George Family Foundation had initially funded several

one-off projects. "We had supported a healing coach position at the Virginia Piper Cancer Institute in Minneapolis and the Healing the Heart initiative at the Minneapolis Heart Institute," Penny explains. "We also helped fund Dr. James Gordon's work at the Center for Mind-Body Medicine in Washington, DC, as well as the work of Dr. Dean Ornish. But our philanthropy was a little here, a little there. What we needed was a strategic plan for broad-based change."

Upon hearing Penny's vision, Diane was immediately on board. "After all the many years that I had been involved in philanthropy and wealth management, it had been my hope to one day help philanthropists work together to bring a meaningful social change project to scale," she says.

As Diane and Penny talked that day, it became clear that what they needed to do first was *convene the people who were already spearheading the call for transformation*. "The idea was to bring the best minds together—the professionals who had confronted the problems in an effective way and the philanthropists who had already supported integrative medicine and would be open to doing more," explains Diane. The question to be answered at the convening: How could the field of integrative medicine be moved forward to accelerate social change?

This convening, which the George Family Foundation planned and funded, was the first step in the effort to effect change on a national level.

Starting with known kindred spirits, Penny and Diane formed a planning committee consisting of themselves, Erminia (Mimi) Guarneri, MD, founder of Scripps Integrative Medicine; Bridget Duffy, MD, then–medical director of Medtronic Foundation; and philanthropic advisor Claire Gaudiani, PhD, then-president of Connecticut College. These five women gathered for a weekend at the George's home in the mountains of Colorado to further develop the idea of a national convening of philanthropic and healthcare leaders involved with integrative medicine.

"Ours was a wide-ranging discussion," explains Diane. "We talked about strategies for how to bring integrative medicine to scale and how to engage the meeting participants so that everyone felt that they had a place at the table. Then Mimi opened up the philosophical quandary of how to get scientists to understand that some of the things which can't be completely understood by science—such as mind and spirit—are critical to healing."

They came to realize that finding the right people would require a great deal of networking, vetting, and strategic selection. But having confirmed the idea of a convening to be in everyone's best interests, the women embraced the challenge.

Penny and Diane would work diligently for the better part of a year to identify the right people and to plan an agenda that would accomplish their goals, set the conversation in an historical context, and provide for a moving experience, with the ultimate goal of securing the participants' commitment to collaborate.

UNCOVERING THE RELATIONSHIP BETWEEN LIFE EVENTS AND HEALTH

About this same time, in Rye, New York, Christy Mack was struggling with a personal crisis while serving on the board of her children's school. "It was affecting my health," she explains. "But I didn't understand how an event could change a person's health. Nobody had hit me over the head with a baseball bat. I hadn't contracted a disease. And yet, I was changing."

One day she looked at herself in the mirror and did not like the reflection she saw. She was irritable and becoming increasingly ill. "That's when I realized that medicine was sorely lacking in its understanding of the relationship between our health, who we are, and all the events that happen in our lives."

Christy immediately embarked on a personal quest to re-examine her whole life. Coincidentally, her husband, John Mack, then-CEO of Morgan Stanley, received a flyer in the mail from Duke University promoting a continuing medical education event. "I did not attend Duke, and John had only been a pre-med student there for one month, so we really shouldn't have received the flyer, but as these things can happen, there it was," Christy explains. "I was fascinated because the flyer had a picture of a religious icon on the cover." Intrigued, Christy decided to find out what kind of medicine they were teaching at Duke.

At the event in Durham, North Carolina, Christy met two physicians—Larry Burk, MD, an oncology radiologist, and Marty Sullivan, MD, a cardiologist—who were interested in mind-body medicine and in caring for the whole person, not just treating the body. The friendship she developed with them was life-changing.

"I think there are different scenarios in our lives that cause us to stop, breathe deeply, and take stock in what we're doing with our lives," she explains. "Sometimes we can lose our relationship with ourselves because we get so wrapped up in everything else that's going on. And then along comes a financial crisis, or a health crisis, or a relationship crisis, and life grinds to a halt. I'm grateful for what happened to me. It afforded me the opportunity to be self-reflective, but it also inspired me to be an active participant with others on the journey and help the journey unfold on a larger level."

In the course of her explorations, Christy saw Andrew Weil on a PBS program. Through connections at PBS, she and John were able to meet him for lunch. "Later, while I was on vacation with my family at Miraval in Tucson, Arizona, I drove down to see Andy's program and give him a check from our family foundation to support his work," Christy explains. "While I was there, he introduced me to Tracy Gaudet, MD, his then–executive director, who helped him develop their fellowship program. (See Chapter Nine.) Tracy and I have been friends ever since."

When Christy returned to New York, she flew back down to Duke to speak with Ralph Snyderman, MD, who at the time was the Chancellor of the Duke University Health System. "You need to know what Andy Weil is doing out in Arizona," she told him.

"There was a lot of networking going on, but it was isolated and on a small scale," Christy explains. So when Penny called and said that she wanted to bring the leading integrative medicine doctors and philanthropists together to talk about changing healthcare through integrative medicine, Christy was quick to respond. "I'm there," she said.

BUILDING A NEW MODEL OF CARE

During this same time period, but unbeknownst to the others, William (Bill) Sarnoff's wife was also diagnosed with cancer. "Like many families that face this problem, we had two years of absolute hell," Bill explains. "We were both blessed and cursed by being in the right zip code, which meant we could get to see almost anyone in healthcare we wanted to see. So for months we ran around the country looking for help at all the supposedly excellent places. No one was a bad guy, but virtually no one gave a damn about my wife other than as a disease to be cured. Nobody considered her as a human being, and towards the end there were some ridiculous things that were proposed and done."

After his wife died, Bill, who was on the Board of Directors of Beth Israel Medical Center in New York City, went to the chairman, Steve Horowitz, MD, and said, "We're doing this wrong, and so is almost everybody else." Bill advocated for a more patient-centered system and for incorporating a more holistic approach. Dr. Horowitz agreed that change was needed.

"You secure the funding, and we'll set up a center," Dr. Horowitz told Bill.

Bill did secure the funding, and in 2000, with the help of Woodson Merrell, MD, and others, the Continuum Center for Health and Healing at Beth Israel (now Mount Sinai Beth Israel) Medical Center in New York City was born. "We were one of the first major urban hospitals to have a center for integrative healthcare," explains Bill. "It wasn't easy to get the money, or to staff it, or to operate within the hospital system, but we did it. And we survived."

Shortly after Continuum opened, Bill received a call from Diane Neimann, asking if she and Penny George could come visit the center. "Diane said that Penny wanted do something on a national level in this area and was convening a group of people to talk about it," Bill explains. "Long story short, they did come to New York—these two extraordinarily smart and impressive people—and when they saw what we were doing at Continuum, they asked me to join them at Miraval." Bill decided to attend.

CHANGING DIRECTIONS

Knowing that she wanted to have a depth of knowledge concerning philanthropy at the meeting, Diane contacted Charles Terry, a colleague who at the time was the director of philanthropy at the Rockefeller Family Office in New York. After telling him about the upcoming gathering at Miraval, she asked him if he would present at one of the breakout sessions. Charles declined, explaining that his wife, Betsy MacGregor, MD—who incidentally worked with Bill Sarnoff at Continuum—was battling breast cancer and that they weren't in a position to do much, because not only was Betsy in the process of treatment, but they had also decided to move to the West Coast.

"But then Diane sent us this lovely article that Penny had written about her journey with cancer," explains Charles. "It was a beautiful essay, and after we read it, we agreed to at least meet Penny."

A dinner was arranged. During the meal, something changed in Charles and Betsy's mind-set. "We had been winding down," Charles says, "and then all of a sudden, we were getting involved in something new."

"That they became an important part of our facilitation process is a testament to the wisdom of our invitation," recalls Penny. "Identifying and engaging the right people has always been key to Bravewell's success."

THE POWER OF NETWORKING

One by one, the right people for the meeting were found. "We basically used a lifetime of connections," Diane comments.

"For instance, I went to see my friend Charlie Halpern at the Nathan Cummings Foundation, one of the funders of the Bill Moyers series, *Healing and the Mind*, because I wanted to talk with him about philanthropic collaboratives," explains Diane. "Charlie introduced me to the other people who had helped fund Bill Moyers' work and also opened the door to our meeting Judith Moyers. Charles Terry put me in touch with Kathleen Foley, MD, who was working for George Soros at the Soros Foundation, and she introduced me to Nancy McCabe from the Kohlberg Foundation. Mimi Guarneri introduced us to Woody Merrell, which is how we found Bill Sarnoff. That's how it worked."

While Diane was concentrating on identifying the philanthropists who might become funders, Penny reached out to the leading healthcare professionals who were working to transform medicine.

IT WAS IN THE AIR

Something was in the air.

"Bravewell was one part of a larger wave," Diane explains. "There was a cultural dynamic coming together at the same time that

Bravewell was coming together. We didn't know it at the time, but the convening at Miraval would help form a strong sense of camaraderie and common purpose among diverse people, many of whom had never met each other before."

"When you set an intention to solve a problem, not just for yourself, but to solve it for other people as well, that sets something powerful in motion," explains Christy. "Which is exactly what happened."

CHAPTER TWO

The Conversation at Miraval

*"Alone we can do so little; together we can
do so much."*

— HELEN KELLER

S UCCESSFUL CONVENINGS—those in which participants come away inspired and through which tangible outcomes emerge—rarely "just happen." For the most part, such meetings are the result of careful planning and preparation, and expert facilitation.

Held April 4–6, 2001, the "Conversation at Miraval" was no exception. Both Penny George and Diane Neimann understood the daunting task in gathering thirty-six prominent leaders together to build consensus and collaboration. "It was an opportunity to leapfrog over the incremental changes that were happening to dream a larger dream," explains Penny. "But we knew such a meeting could easily go awry, so we spent a good amount of time thinking about process."

"We both believed that if we brought together the right people—people with good hearts and minds—around a shared vision, with effective facilitation, then good things would inevitably happen," adds Penny. "And they did."

One of the most important aspects of their pre-work was to have everyone embrace a common vision, lest the meeting itself be wasted discussing what integrative medicine was, rather than how it could be advanced. To help foster that common vision, the planning committee sent out questionnaires in advance, the first question of which was: What is your vision of integrative medicine? They distributed the answers ahead of time and made consensus statements on poster boards for the actual meeting.

"It worked well," Penny explains. "We had a clarity of vision from the beginning."

THE ORIGINAL CONSENSUS STATEMENT

Integrative medicine seeks to integrate the best of conventional medicine with:

✳ A broader understanding of the nature of illness and wellness

✳ The role of factors such as mind, spirit, culture, and caring

✳ The importance of partnership between the patient and physician/other healthcare providers in treatment and recovery

✳ Those complementary treatment modalities that have been best shown to add value.

IT'S NOT ABOUT THE HORSE

The Miraval gathering began at the Kiva Pit with a Tibetan bowl meditation orchestrated by integrative oncologist Mitch Gaynor, MD, and a welcome by Wyatt Webb, a tall man dressed in cowboy gear who explained that he would be leading the group through a unique equine experience the following morning.

During a Miraval equine exercise, a participant enters the corral in which there is one horse. The objective is for that person to get the horse to lift its hoof to be cleaned. It is not as easy as one might think, as the horse is trained to sense fear, doubt, and hesitation, and generally only lifts its leg when the person's intention is strong and clear. Once successful, participants come away with a good understanding that it (life) is not about the horse—it's about them.

The next morning, several people in the group volunteered to participate while everyone else looked on. "You can be out there for hours trying to get this horse to lift its hoof," Diane remembers. "Most of the people became frustrated, and one was even reduced to tears."

When his turn came, John Mack, then–CEO and chairman of the board of Morgan Stanley, started walking across the open space towards the horse. And before he even got to the horse, the horse put its foot up.

"It just shows you what can happen when your intention is set," laughs Diane.

SHARING PERSONAL STORIES

Before engaging in the brainstorming process, Penny and Diane arranged to have a few pre-selected people tell their personal stories of what brought them to value integrative medicine. As these stories were told, it became self-evident that many of the elements critical to healing—such as love and compassion—were beyond the scope of conventional medicine and defied measurement by science.

SMALL GROUPS, BIG IDEAS

Several times during the Miraval meeting, the participants were divided up into small groups to talk about the key determinants of the future of medicine. The individual discussions were thoughtful and far-ranging. Then, through a series of facilitated exercises, the participants came back together, shared their ideas, and agreed upon four focused strategies for furthering the adoption of integrative medicine. These were to:

❊ Create a critical mass of university/academic health centers working in collaboration to develop, research, and teach all aspects of integrative medicine

❊ Establish core values for the transformation of human health by emphasizing humanism, self-care, and the sacred bond between patients, physicians, and other healthcare workers

❊ Create a redefinition of public health that embraces the spirit, values, and knowledge of integrative medicine

❊ Organize a philanthropic community to accelerate change through collaborative efforts.

"One of the principles that emerged from the discussions, which would underlie all our work, was to give the field more credibility by working with physicians first," explains Diane. "We knew if we couldn't get physicians on board, the healthcare system would never fully embrace integrative medicine." Put in different words, the participants felt that the transformation would happen faster if it came from the inside; hence, their tactic was *to partner with the very system they wished to change.*

Two other core principles the philanthropists adopted were: (1) *Don't reinvent the wheel,* meaning that if something is being done well by others, don't duplicate it—partner with them instead; and (2) *Create synergy,* meaning that whenever possible, and if it fit the mission and vision, help advance change that was already in the process of emerging.

BEING HEARD

One of the processes that Penny and Diane used to keep the Miraval meeting flowing smoothly and on track was to take copious notes during the day, synthesize them after hours, and then slip an executive summary under everyone's door that night.

"We wanted people to know we heard what they had to say and that we were taking their comments seriously," explains Penny.

GROUNDED IN VALUES

An overarching value that drove the design and execution of the meeting was that it should be a shared experience and a shared dialogue. Everyone would have a chance to talk, but not about themselves or their own work. The conversation would focus solely on the goal of moving integrative medicine forward.

Because of this, "the physicians and the philanthropists took off their hats," explains Bill George. "They weren't identified as *this doctor* or *that philanthropist*, but as people who were committed to the same goal. It was that mutuality of goals, that shared purpose and shared set of values, that made the difference."

As Woody Merrell, MD, relates, "The process worked brilliantly. It took a very diverse group with many interests, agendas, and ideas and produced a clear set of goals in two days."

ACTION EMERGES

Another specific "rule" set in advance for the meeting was that no one would solicit the philanthropists for funding during the meeting. And no one did, at least not wittingly.

Toward the end of the Miraval meeting, Ralph Snyderman, MD, then–chancellor for health affairs and dean of the Duke University School of Medicine, was asked what he thought was crucial to moving the field forward. He answered that from his perspective, the most important thing was to have enough funding to bring the members of the newly-formed Academic Consortium together again so they could create a plan as to how, through their universities, they could change medicine. He explained that about a year earlier, representatives from a handful of academic medical institutions had convened a historic meeting at the Fetzer Institute in Kalamazoo, Michigan. The participating institutions all had significant experience and interest in the field of integrative medicine as well as high-level support from their leadership. Their goal was to create a formal consortium that would work to advance integrative medicine.

John Mack asked how much money it would take to facilitate that work, and Ralph told him $500,000 over five years. Without a second thought to the rules, John answered, "We can do that." While some of the philanthropists in the room objected to any commitment of funds, John and Christy Mack, Bill and Penny George, and Ron Mannix pledged their full support, and so it began—connections had been made, passions had been shared, a vision had emerged, and the collaborative work had begun.

OUTCOMES

"I think one of the most important outcomes of the first Miraval meeting was the link that was established between the physicians and the philanthropists," explains Bill George. "*A sense of oneness* was generated because the discussion was about mutually shared goals."

"By asking key questions, we carefully orchestrated a conversation in which people shared their thoughts about the future," explains Diane. "Where would the group like integrative medicine to be in ten years? What was possible? What were the main obstacles? It was an envisioning exercise that, in terms of commitment and ideas, was participated in equally by the practitioners and the philanthropists."

"In my experience, that is unique," adds Bill George. "Normally, you have the people doing the work presenting their ideas and vision to the philanthropists. In this case, it was jointly derived from a blank sheet of paper. I think it was very powerful that *everyone in the meeting had an equal voice.*"

"The first Miraval meeting was the only time, up to that point, that we had philanthropists coming together with physicians, all of whom were looking to transform healthcare," adds Mimi Guarneri, MD. "That partnership was one of the first times that I had ever witnessed a group of philanthropists looking to use their resources *to create a movement* as opposed to just benefit one isolated center or one small area."

Two important outcomes emerged from the Miraval meeting. First, a subgroup was created to oversee the funding needed to support the infrastructure of the nascent Academic Consortium for Integrative Medicine & Health. And second, the philanthropists agreed to meet again to continue the conversation.

INTEGRATIVE HEALTH LEADERS AT MIRAVAL I

Brian Berman, MD, *University of Maryland School of Medicine*

Bridget Duffy, MD, *Medtronic, Inc.*

David Eisenberg, MD, *Beth Israel Deaconess Medical Center*

Tracy Gaudet, MD, *Duke Medical Center*

Mitchell Gaynor, MD, *Cornell Center for Complementary and Integrative Medicine*

Jeremy Geffen, MD, *Geffen Cancer Center and Research Institute*

James Gordon, MD, *Center for Mind Body Medicine*

Erminia Guarneri, MD, *Scripps Center for Integrative Medicine*

Jon Kabat-Zinn, PhD, *University of Massachusetts Medical School*

Betsy MacGregor, MD, *Beth Israel Medical Center*

Woodson Merrell, MD, *Beth Israel Medical Center*

Dean Ornish, MD, *Preventive Medicine Research Institute*

Mehmet Oz, MD, *Columbia University/New York Presbyterian Hospital*

Kenneth Pelletier, PhD, *Stanford University School of Medicine*

Gregory Plotnikoff, MD, *University of Minnesota Center for Spirituality and Healing*

Ralph Snyderman, MD, *Duke Medical Center*

David Strand, *Allina Health Systems*

Marty Sullivan, MD, *Duke Medical Center*

Val Ulstad, MD, MPH, *Bush Foundation Leadership Board*

Andrew Weil, MD, *University of Arizona*

PHILANTHROPIC AND FOUNDATION LEADERS AT MIRAVAL I

Anne Bartley, *Rockefeller Family Fund*

Berkley Bedell, *National Foundation for Alternative Medicine*

Kathy Davison, *Citibank (Philanthropic Services)*

Penny George, PsyD, *The George Family Foundation*

William (Bill) George, *The George Family Foundation*

Charles Halpern, *Philanthropic Advisor*

Sandra Lund, *The Soros Charitable Foundation*

Christy Mack, *Philanthropist*

John Mack, *Philanthropist*

Ron Mannix, *Coril Holdings, Ltd.*

Nancy McCabe, *The Kohlberg Foundation*

Diane Neimann, *Family Philanthropy Advisors*

Ellen Pomeroy, *Advisor to Laurence S. Rockefeller*

William (Bill) Sarnoff, *Philanthropist*

John Templeton, *The John Templeton Foundation*

Charles Terry, *Philanthropic Advisor*

FACILITATOR

Claire Gaudiani, PhD

CHAPTER THREE

Pocantico: Bold Decisions

❦

"Collective wisdom reflects a similar capacity to learn together and evolve toward something greater and wiser than what we can do as individuals alone. It emerges from a deep conviction that we have a stake in each other and that what binds us together is greater than what drives us apart."

— **ALAN BRISKIN**

T HE GERMAN WRITER AND PHILOSOPHER Goethe once said, "Concerning all acts of initiative and creation, there is one elementary truth the ignorance of which kills countless ideas and splendid plans: that the moment one definitely commits oneself, then providence moves too. All sorts of things occur to help one that would never otherwise have occurred... Whatever you can do or dream you can do, begin it. Boldness has genius, power and magic in it."

Boldness is an appropriate word to describe the decisions that were made at the second meeting of philanthropists on November 7–9, 2001 at the Pocantico Conference Center of the Rockefeller Brothers Fund in Westchester County, New York. As it will become clear in later chapters, committing to a course of action set a future in motion that at the time, no one, not even the most optimistic, could have imagined.

PREPARATION

First, staging the meeting at the Pocantico Center was a strategic choice because doing so would signify a certain level of recognition from the Rockefeller Brothers Fund. The application process for a grant from this fund is rigorous. The Fund "advances social change that contributes to a more just, sustainable, and peaceful world" and its programs are intended to "develop leaders, strengthen institutions, engage citizens, build community, and foster partnerships that include government, business, and civil society."

"In order to be invited to convene at Pocantico, you must demonstrate that your group meets the Rockefeller's standards for innovation and leadership," explains Diane Neimann. "If your proposal is successful then you are awarded everything you need to make your conference a success—great facilities, meals, equipment, and support staff."

Bravewell's application was approved.

Second, the objective of the Pocantico gathering was to explore the possibility of creating a sustainable collaboration among philanthropists, so the invitation list included only philanthropists and only those who might be inclined to get involved. Again, process played a crucial role in the meeting's success.

"Getting started on the right track was critical," explains Bill George. "It's like the Dalai Lama once said about sending a rocket ship to the moon. If you are off by one degree, you miss the moon by 10,000 miles."

Penny and Diane worked with Charles Terry, who would facilitate the meeting, to create a set of operating principles that would engender success. "It was values like collegiality, collaboration, and the idea that no one would advocate for their own projects, but instead stay focused on what the group could do as a team to advance the field, that really made a difference," Diane explains.

"Additionally, in planning the Pocantico meeting, we knew it would only work if we could get people out of their everyday roles and everyday selves and into a more creative, right-brain place with deeper connections to themselves and others," says Charles. "So we planned activities that would encourage that shift. If you have the right soil, the plant will grow."

Building on what had been accomplished at the first meeting at Miraval, clear goals for the meeting were established:

⁕   To build a sense of community among those involved

⁕   To harvest the collective experience and wisdom

⁕   To coalesce around a few select strategic ideas that would make a significant difference

⁕   To plan collaborative action steps for moving forward.

"We communicated that the gathering was a collective inquiry, a search for common ground on which together we might create something new that would make a significant difference," says Diane. Penny adds that she, Diane, and Charles firmly believe "there is greater wisdom in the group than in any one individual."

GUIDELINES FOR A SUCCESSFUL CONVERSATION

Show up/be present

Listen deeply

Speak your truth

Be open to new ideas and different perspectives

Respect each person's voice

Don't rush to find answers

Hold the differences, the paradoxes, and the multiple truths

Honor the quiet spaces where creativity can enter

Maintain a sense of humor/lightness

Engage all aspects of intelligence—mind, heart, intuition

Respect privacy

Welcome the unexpected

Don't be attached to outcomes

Trust/open your heart

THE PARTICIPANTS

Not every philanthropist who attended Miraval I, as it has come to be known, chose to return to the next meeting. Some self-selected out, while others were networked in.

"There were some wonderful people who came to the early sessions, such as Bernard Osher, who simply aren't one to be part of any group," comments Bill George. "The Osher Foundation funds select integrative medicine centers on their own, and that is very important work."

People's choices were respected. "Bravewell was only one piece of a larger effort to change medicine," adds Bill.

THE WEB OF CONNECTIONS

During this time, the Lovell Family Foundation was engaged in the philanthropic support of mental health and integrative medicine, especially around the issues of arthritis, cancer, and cancer survivorship in both Ohio, where the Lovell family had lived for many years, and Arizona, where Lu and her daughter Ann had moved following the death of Mr. Lovell.

One day, Lu received a call from the development director at the University of Toledo, who proved to be one of those unforeseen and unwitting "assistants to the cause." The development director was simply calling to touch base and find out what the Lovell Foundation had been engaged in recently. Lu told her that the foundation was excited about integrative medicine. According to Lu, "When my husband was still alive we had a practitioner work with him using meditation and guided imagery. He was an engineer, a just-the-facts kind of guy, but he took to it, and the quality of his last days was remarkable. I became a believer after that."

Upon hearing this, the development director told Lu that she needed to meet her best friend from childhood, because this friend, whose name was Penny George, was also involved with integrative medicine. This "coincidence" led Lu and Ann to attend the Pocantico meeting and join Bravewell.

RIVERS OF LIFE

"The meeting at Pocantico was designed to open up our thinking to the full array of possible ideas and strategies," explains Diane. "Then, guided by the collective experience and wisdom of the group, to let that thinking coalesce, and then choose two or three specific strategies to generate change."

Activities for the first day focused on building a sense of community among the philanthropists, including the sharing of personal stories and a long discussion about the nature of healing. It culminated with everyone drawing their own "river of life" in which they depicted those life events that caused them to be deeply interested in health and healing.

The idea behind the "river of life" exercise is to find a larger context of the flow of one's life and enable people to connect deeply around life experiences that led them to this point. "You have people draw the milestones, but it is not a review. The idea is to find out where your life is going, because, through the touchstones, it becomes obvious that if you become this and do that, new possibilities will open up," explains Charles. "Afterwards, everyone sits in a circle, shows their river picture, and talks about it. It's a magical process."

The exercise is designed to help people delve into the direction and purpose of their lives. "We wanted people to make strategic decisions from that deeper place," adds Charles.

"I will never forget sitting on the floor next to Berkley Bedell, Bruce Dayton, and Bernard Osher as we all drew our rivers of life on these large pieces of paper," says Christy Mack. "When we were all done, we discovered the most amazing thing—all of our rivers went upstream. Everyone in the room had drawn themselves as fighting the current."

LOSING YOUR SUITCASE

In her travels to get to Pocantico, Betsy MacGregor, MD, lost her suitcase. But instead of looking at it as a bad thing, she saw the metaphor in play. "Losing your suitcase became a theme at the meeting. It meant leaving behind all the things we don't need to carry along with us," Betsy explains. "We were all going somewhere new."

COLLABORATION

The next two days were spent on identifying and developing those strategies that would make the most difference in the transformation of healthcare.

"The first question was: Could we develop collaboration among philanthropists?" explains Diane. "Because we knew that none of the other strategies would ever be implemented unless we had a strong core group of philanthropists who were inspired, and committed, and could work together."

"My fondest hope was that people would see that we could accomplish so much more together than we could ever accomplish individually," adds Penny.

Pocantico was the turning point. A true sense of community was emerging, and as it did, a collective vision began to form. A decision was made to fully embrace the idea of working together, and the group charged Diane with developing a business proposal to form an "integrative medicine funding collaborative" that would be set up as an operating foundation, not a grant-making organization. The collaborative would choose, fund, and manage its own initiatives. This would prove to be one of Bravewell's most important strategic decisions, as it set the stage for continued shared visioning, personal involvement, and a culture of partnerships.

Key behaviors for success were identified:

✳ Build trust

✳ Set clear goals

✳ Find common ground

✳ Invite participation

✳ Evaluate regularly

✳ Keep donors informed and involved

✳ Nurture relationships, meaning, and community.

"One of the first things we did right was actually something we didn't do," adds Christy. "And what we didn't do was let the fear of the unknown keep us from doing what we knew had to be done. We were talking about things that were way up in the ethers, and we had no idea how we were going to pull it all down to earth or convey it to the nation. How were we going to manifest this vision? We didn't know, and that fear of the unknown was huge. Social change isn't easy, and it is very expensive. But we were bold, and we found strength in the community we were forming. We discovered that refusing to be shackled by fears or doubts was really what enabled us to move forward."

NO GREEN BANANAS
As the group began to hone in on which strategies would create the desired change, Bill Sarnoff announced that he had something important to say. "No green bananas."

Over the years, those three words became a Bravewell watchword. The expression means choose initiatives that will ripen—produce results—in a relatively short time span. It also implies maintaining a sense of urgency—time is money, especially when resources are limited.

In that spirit, the philanthropists agreed upon three strategies that could move the field forward:

* Change the culture within medicine
  Work to change the way physicians are educated and recognize and support integrative medicine physician leaders

* Map the Field
  Develop a broad understanding of the forces at work in the emergence of integrative medicine, and document the existing landscape

* Develop successful models of integrative care
  Identify and support a small network of successful integrative medicine centers that could serve as centers of excellence for others to emulate.

After work assignments were made to research how those three strategies might be implemented, the next meeting was set for six months later, on May 15–17, 2002 at Miraval in Tucson, Arizona.

POCANTICO PHILANTHROPISTS

Dorothy Beckwith, *Beckwith Family Foundation*

Berkley Bedell, *National Foundation for Alternative Medicine*

Bruce B. Dayton, *Philanthropist*

Ruth Stricker Dayton, *Philanthropist*

Bridget Duffy, MD, *Medtronic, Inc.*

Phyllis Farley, *Philanthropist*

Kathleen Foley, MD, *The Open Society Institute*

Penny George, PsyD, *The George Family Foundation*

William (Bill) George, *The George Family Foundation*

Lucy Gonda, *Lucy Gonda Foundation*

Glenda Greenwald, *Philanthropist*

Michael Hill, *Memensha Fund of the Dorot Foundation*

Ann Lovell, *The Lovell Foundation*

Lu Lovell, *The Lovell Foundation*

Christy Mack, *Christy and John Mack Foundation*

Nancy McCabe, *The Kohlberg Foundation*

Diane Neimann, *The George Family Foundation*

Bernard Osher, *The Bernard Osher Foundation*

Susan Samueli, *Samueli Foundation*

William (Bill) Sarnoff, *Philanthropist*

POCANTICO FACILITATORS

Betsy MacGregor, MD

Charles Terry

CHAPTER FOUR

Miraval II:
Bravewell is Born

"*Follow your bliss and don't be afraid,
and doors will open where you didn't know
they were going to be.*"

— JOSEPH CAMPBELL

THE WORD "WATERSHED" MEANS an event or period marking a turning point in a course of action or state of affairs after which things will never be the same. The birth of Bravewell was just such an event.

The "Philanthropic Collaborative for Integrative Medicine" was officially founded as an operating foundation on April 4, 2002. (The name was changed in 2006 to The Bravewell Collaborative.) With this formal incorporation, the George Family Foundation, which had provided both funding and leadership for the two previous meetings, "passed the baton" to the group as a whole.

Penny George, Bill Sarnoff, and Christy Mack were named as the incorporating board of directors and Diane Neimann was named executive director. Under their leadership, members gathered at Miraval to begin establishing the organizational structures that would enable Bravewell's mission to be realized.

IMPORTANT FOUNDING DECISIONS

Wishing to fund strategic initiatives of its own choosing, The Bravewell Collaborative had been deliberately established as a 501(c)(3) *operating* foundation rather than a grant-making one. "Three distinctions were central to our planning," explains Penny George. "We said the organization must be *funder-driven* and *participatory* and that it should *initiate* rather than react."

The group instituted two financial requirements for membership:

(1) a minimum gift of $100,000 over three years to support general operations, which would later rise to $150,000, and (2) an additional major gift supporting at least one of the chosen initiatives. Wishing to protect and enhance the emerging philanthropic community, the leadership also set other requirements. New members would need to have a strong interest in integrative medicine, possess the ability to work collaboratively, exhibit a generosity of spirit, and be a cultural fit with the existing membership.

"One of the most important decisions we made at Miraval II was that everyone who met the minimum monetary commitment for membership would have an equal voice at the table," explains Diane Neimann. "Those donating $100,000 had the same stature as those donating $1 million." This simple decision set the stage for true collaboration and an atmosphere of mutual respect.

The group set a funding goal of $10 million over ten years. By the end of the Miraval II meeting, Bravewell had raised $4.36 million.

OPERATING PRINCIPLES

During Bravewell's formation process, Diane purposely reconnected with colleagues in the philanthropic community who had extensive experience in working with a variety of collaborative efforts. "Kathy Foley's work in pain and palliative care through the Soros Foundation made her a valuable advisor," says Diane. "Charles Halpern at the Cummings Foundation had related experience with the sponsorship of the Moyers PBS series, as did Nancy McCabe at the Kohlberg Foundation."

This networking with philanthropic advisors uncovered that *shared values* topped the list of requirements for success.

Consequently, during the second Miraval meeting, the group was asked to think about values and operating principles. The work wasn't just about establishing legal bylaws, it was also about understanding how to deal with each other and with the inevitable problems that would arise.

Important principles that were embraced:

✳ A shared vision

✳ Dedication to the mission

✳ Clear and achievable goals.

CAREFULLY CHOSEN INITIATIVES

Bravewell's strategies for creating change were the result of a group process. "Because one of our key principles was that everybody's voice mattered, the initiatives we finally settled on were the summation of all of our thinking together. I believe people support what they help to create, and the group's steadfast commitment to the goals and values were reflective of that," explains Penny.

This perspective also helped shape Bravewell's overarching strategy of supporting and partnering with the people and institutions that were already doing the work.

"When you think about our initiatives, it is important to remember that our goal was to change the entire healthcare system, not just a piece of it," says Ann Lovell. "So for us, it wasn't about who could practice acupuncture or how to improve reimbursement for massage. Those kinds of questions would get answered as the new system emerged. Our question was about how we could create broad-based, fundamental change."

"Our most important strategy was to be driven by the vision that was integrative medicine and to create initiatives in support of that vision," adds Christy Mack. "Ergo, we only funded the vision, we did not fund one specific institution or individual or agenda."

Informed by the work of previous meetings, the philanthropists approved these five formal initiatives:

* Grow a dynamic community of committed and informed philanthropists

* Change the way physicians are educated

* Document the existing landscape

* Empower and support physician champions

* Accelerate the growth of leading clinical centers in integrative medicine.

ARTICULATING INHERENT VALUES

Knowing it was important to have a document that they could share with others as their initiatives moved forward, the philanthropists worked to articulate the new medicine they wanted to see emerge.

"We knew that the relationships between patients and their physicians and their other healthcare providers needed to be reconfigured. Patients should be active partners in their own care, not just recipients of instructions," says Bill Sarnoff.

"People needed to be empowered to be the principal agents of their own health and to be offered real choices in their healing," Penny adds.

According to Lu Lovell, "It was also imperative that we facilitate a deep understanding of the role of mind, body, community, and spirit in healing. And not just with the providers. We wanted the whole healthcare system to embrace the connections."

"We understood that the transformation should include broad acceptance of preventive strategies," adds Christy. "Health is the most importance asset any of us have, so in addition to curing disease and handling trauma, the system also needed to promote health."

After many discussions and under Christy's guidance, the

members created a "Declaration for a New Medicine." It was toward the adoption of these principles that The Bravewell Collaborative would direct its future efforts.

DECLARATION FOR A NEW MEDICINE

✳ We value the treatment of the individual in a holistic manner and the fulfillment of the needs of mind, body, and spirit.

✳ We recognize the sacred and healing nature of the relationships between patients and healthcare providers and acknowledge that humanism, compassion, and caring are central to health and healing.

✳ We believe that the empowered patient is the responsible central actor in healing, self-care, and prevention and that a person's emotions, trauma, and stress levels directly affect the risk and course of disease.

✳ We will work for a healthcare system which creates an environment that supports healing relationships and recognizes that in order to be healing and empowering, healers themselves must be restored and whole.

✳ We will support truly integrative medicine that offers the highest standards of excellence in a full and complete array of evidence-based care modalities.

✳ We embrace the spiritual dimension of life and acknowledge the importance of context and intention in the healing process for patients, caregivers, and healers.

✳ We acknowledge that the risks of many serious illnesses, such as cancer, cardiovascular disease, and diabetes, can be reduced with scientifically-based nutrition, exercise, and mind-body interventions.

✳   We believe in giving voice to the patient, in the openness
of healers, and in honest and supportive communications
among all members of the healthcare community.

✳   We will support the efforts of healers to develop the integrity
and spiritual qualities that are as important as medical
knowledge and technical skills to the process of healing.

✳   We dedicate ourselves to the change necessary to bring
about the new medicine in an optimal healing environment.

MIRAVAL II PARTICIPANTS

Dorothy Beckwith, *Beckwith Family Foundation*

Berkley Bedell, *National Foundation for Alternative Medicine*

Ira Brind, *Philanthropist*

Myrna Brind, *Philanthropist*

Georgine Busch, *The Earl and Doris Bakken Foundation*

Paul Gailey, *The Fetzer Institute*

Penny George, PsyD, *The George Family Foundation*

William (Bill) George, *The George Family Foundation*

Lucy Gonda, *Lucy Gonda Foundation*

Gerald Greenwald, *Former CEO, United Airlines*

Glenda Greenwald, *Aspen Center for New Medicine*

Ann Lovell, *The Lovell Foundation*

Lu Lovell, *The Lovell Foundation*

Christy Mack, *Christy and John Mack Foundation*

Nancy McCabe, *The Kohlberg Foundation*

Diane Neimann, *The George Family Foundation*

William (Bill) Sarnoff, *Philanthropist*

CHAPTER FIVE

Choosing the Right Language

❧

"The content of every culture is expressible in its language."

— EDWARD SAPIR

I N HIS BOOK, *CULTURE AND LANGUAGE*, B. Otto states that, "The power of language to reflect culture and influence thinking was first proposed by an American linguist and anthropologist, Edward Sapir, and his student, Benjamin Whorf. The Sapir–Whorf hypothesis stated that *the way we think and view the world is determined by our language.*"

Sapir himself wrote, "Language is heuristic … in the far reaching sense that its forms predetermine for us certain modes of observation and interpretation." In fact, it has been said that when people learn a second language, they also learn a second way to understand the world.

Recognizing the power of language to shape perception, The Bravewell Collaborative gave a good deal of thought as to how integrative medicine should be defined.

The inspiration for the movement had come from many different scientific fields and cultural traditions. For example, the idea that a person should be treated in his or her wholeness—mind, body, and spirit—is a fundamental premise within integrative medicine that has been informed by the patient-centered care movement, biopsychosocial medicine, traditional Chinese medicine, Ayurvedic medicine, indigenous medicine, and the medical traditions of the ancient Greeks as well as consciousness studies and modern humanistic and transpersonal psychology. Prevention and wellness, two other important aspects of integrative medicine, are grounded in medical science, but they also draw from the fields of nutrition, eastern philosophy, sports medicine, and environmental health, among others. The field was essentially a "gathering" of human wisdom in an effort to care for individuals in the best way possible.

While the people involved in integrative medicine shared a common purpose, everyone had a slightly different take on what this new medicine should be, how it should be defined and practiced, and what credentials should be required for those delivering the care. There were many different terms being used to describe what was emerging—words such as "alternative," "integral," "complementary," "blended," "holistic," "integrative," and "cross-cultural." Bravewell understood that finding common ground as well as the right language to express it would be imperative to forward progress.

THE CORE VALUES

The work to establish a common definition began with the very first conversation at Miraval as that group identified the core values held by the field.

"We also made a deliberate decision at Miraval and then reaffirmed it at Pocantico that we would define integrative medicine in the context of public health," explains Christy Mack. "We said that an integrative approach needed to include diet, lifestyle, exercise, and minimization of environmental hazards as well as address the whole person—mind–body–spirit—and that *these values should be held not only by individual practitioners, but also by the health systems in which the practitioners worked.*"

"We wanted integrative medicine to be embraced as a way to ensure the health of the American public," Christy adds. "So our vision wasn't just about what happened in hospitals or clinics. It was also about what happened in homes, schools, offices, and communities. That meant empowering people to participate in safeguarding their own health."

WHAT IS HEALING?

At the Pocantico meeting, the philanthropists engaged in a lengthy conversation about healing and what actually happened when someone was "healed." Each person wrote their definition on a piece of paper and then taped it to a common wall. The "banner" that resulted included the concepts of empowerment, balance, love, compassion, wholeness, and hope.

"We agreed that healing was different from curing," explains Penny George. "Curing is what medical science does through treatment. It's about eliminating the disease or trauma. And even though a practitioner might guide the process, healing is an internal activity that people do for themselves. It's about restoring harmony to the body, mind, and spirit. You can cure without healing, and you can heal without curing, but we thought that healthcare needed to do both."

Another tenet the group embraced was that every person possesses a significant, innate capacity for self-healing that can be supported and enhanced, and that a primary goal of integrative medicine should be to maximize this capacity.

GATHERING ABOVE THE FRAY

Bravewell's strategy was to rise above the territorial struggles and define the field, not in terms of modalities, disciplines, or interventions, but in broad philosophical approaches. For instance, instead of talking about meditation, breathing, or biofeedback to reduce stress, Bravewell talked about addressing the mental and emotional influences that affected health. The "how" was left to the individual practitioner's discernment. One of the benefits of this approach was that it meant that as the science developed, if one modality did not meet the evidence criteria and fell out of use, or if a new modality came into practice, these circumstances did not change the integrative approach to care or its definition.

THE DEFINITION

After years of thoughtful deliberation, Bravewell began using the following definition of integrative medicine:

Integrative medicine is an approach to care that puts the patient at the center and addresses the full range of physical, emotional, mental, social, spiritual, and environmental influences that affect a person's health. Employing a personalized strategy that considers the patient's unique conditions, needs, and circumstances, it uses the most appropriate interventions from an array of scientific disciplines to heal illness and disease and help people regain and maintain optimum health.

In addition to addressing and handling the individual's immediate health problem(s) as well as the deeper causes of the disease or illness, integrative strategies also empower the patient and foster the development of healthy behaviors and skills for effective self-care that people can use throughout their lives.

DEFINING PRINCIPLES

The definition of integrative medicine embraced by Bravewell was informed by the work of practitioners and scholars in the Bravewell Clinical Network (see Chapter Eight), the Center for Integrative Medicine at the University of Arizona (see Chapter Nine), and the Academic Consortium for Integrative Medicine & Health (see Chapter Six). These principles are:

✳ The patient and practitioner are partners in the healing process

✳ All factors that influence health, wellness, and disease are taken into consideration

✳ The care addresses the whole person, including body, mind, and spirit in the context of community

✳ Practitioners use all appropriate healing sciences to facilitate the body's innate healing response

✳ Effective interventions that are natural and less invasive are used whenever possible

✳ Because good medicine is based in good science, integrative medicine is inquiry-driven and open to new models of care

✳ Alongside the concept of treatment, the broader concepts of health promotion and the prevention of illness are paramount

✳ Care is individualized to best address the person's unique conditions, needs, and circumstances

✳ Practitioners of integrative medicine exemplify its principles and commit themselves to self-exploration and self-development.

THE RIGHT NAME

Another linguistic challenge arose around Bravewell's original name—The Philanthropic Collaborative for Integrative Medicine. It was too long and did not capture the spirit of the group. So a committee consisting of Bill Sarnoff, Lynn Getz, and Nancy McCabe was formed and charged with finding a more inspiring name. After considering more than forty words that could describe the effort, the name "The Bravewell Collaborative" emerged.

"It is not the name of a person, but rather the combination of two words—*brave* and *well*—that we believe express the essence of integrative medicine," explains Christy Mack.

The willingness to step forward and take charge—knowing there will be obstacles and adversity as well as successes and rewards—requires strength of character. It takes commitment to swim against the tide and pursue a dream or goal regardless of the risks or the amount of effort involved.

"Integrative medicine would not exist today had it not been for the efforts of the many healthcare leaders who put their reputations on the line and took enormous risks to stand up for their beliefs and change the system," adds Christy. "These values—commitment, courage, leadership, and strength—are celebrated by our choice of the word *brave*."

Why people take these risks, what it is that they so value, is *wellness*. Bravewell members firmly believed that achieving wellness, staying well, and recovering wellness when it is lost is what integrative medicine strives for, and is what each person deserves.

CHAPTER SIX

Change from Within

"Do not follow where the path may lead.
Go instead where there is no path
and leave a trail."

— RALPH WALDO EMERSON

S ELF-ORGANIZED NETWORKS AND CLUSTERS of kindred spirits aren't the whole story of how social change comes into being. Margaret Wheatley advises, "As networks grow and transform into active, working communities of practice, we discover how Life truly changes, which is through *emergence*. When separate, local efforts connect with each other as networks, then strengthen as *communities of practice*, suddenly and surprisingly a new system emerges at a greater level of scale."

Importantly, the new *system of influence* will possess qualities and capacities that were previously unknown.

"It isn't that they were hidden; they simply don't exist until the system emerges," Wheatley explains. "They are properties of the system, not the individual, but once there, individuals possess them. And the system that emerges always possesses greater power and influence than is possible through planned, incremental change. Emergence is how Life creates radical change and takes things to scale."

THE ACADEMIC CONSORTIUM COMES INTO BEING
In July 1999, leadership from eight academic medical institutions met at the Fetzer Institute in Kalamazoo, Michigan, to discuss the idea of forming a network of medical schools interested in advancing

integrative medicine. Representatives from Duke, Harvard, Stanford, University of Arizona, University of Maryland, University of Massachusetts, University of Minnesota, and the University of California, San Francisco, were in attendance.

The idea for the gathering originated with Jon Kabat-Zinn, PhD. He had observed that in a scattering of academic institutions across the nation, isolated activities were taking place that were aimed at changing the way medicine was practiced and the way health was understood. He thought these independent endeavors might be helped by a collaborative, coordinated effort on the part of medical school leadership.

"The idea was to gather the chancellors of medical centers where significant undertakings in developing mind-body and integrative medicine were being made and have them meet on an occasional basis, along with their respective institution's head of the integrative program," explains Jon. The intent was that, during these meetings, strategies for advancing integrative medicine would be discussed, developed, and ultimately initiated.

Jon called Tracy Gaudet, MD, then–executive director of the University of Arizona Program in Integrative Medicine, and solicited her help in organizing the meeting. Through Jon's connections, they were able to secure the Fetzer Institute's retreat center, Gilchrist, as the meeting's venue.

As it turned out, the gathering at Fetzer proved to be unique on many levels. One of the requirements was that participants had to bring the highest medical official in the healthcare system with them, which was very unusual. Additionally, at the time of the meeting, Michigan was in the midst of an extreme heat wave and the air conditioning at the Fetzer retreat center had failed, so it was very hot. Throwing formalities out the window, the participants ended up taking off their shoes and socks. When the electricity went out, the remainder of the meeting was conducted by candlelight.

"The heat and the failed lights acted like a disorienting dilemma," reflects Mary Jo Kreitzer, RN, PhD, founder and director of the Center for Spirituality and Healing at the University of Minnesota. Referencing transformational learning literature, she adds that, "It caused us all to let go of a lot of preconceived ideas about what should or should not be happening, and to shift our thinking and perspectives, and truly meet the moment."

By the time of the first Miraval meeting with the philanthropists, the Fetzer group had coalesced into a small but committed community.

A PLEDGE OF SUPPORT

The most critical need identified by the physicians who attended Miraval I was for fundamental change in the core curriculum for medical students at leading academic institutions. It had become clear to the philanthropists that no matter what else they accomplished, changing medical education and training was essential to sustain the movement toward integrative medicine.

"Segmentation of medicine into specialties, overemphasis on technology and pharmaceuticals, and ignorance of prevention strategies and of complementary modalities that had been shown to add value were just some of the barriers that needed to be overcome in the training of physicians and other healthcare professionals," explains Ralph Snyderman, MD, now chancellor emeritus of Duke University.

But doing so would be a significant undertaking. "We knew that real change would take time because it would require reorientation of the organizational cultures of established institutions," adds Ralph. "That's never easy. However, wide-scale effects would be felt when the medical students who learned within the revised curricula were established in practice."

After the Macks, Ron Mannix, and the Georges pledged their support to fund continued meetings of the fledging Academic Consortium, the philanthropists asked the group's founders to develop a plan and an organizational structure that would truly build the capacity to change the way physicians were educated in major academic health centers.

"It fit nicely with our strategy to get behind and support the people who were already out front and doing the work," remarks Diane Neimann.

When Brian Berman, MD, and Tracy Gaudet, MD, presented the formal plan to create the Academic Consortium for Integrative Medicine & Health as a 501(c)(3) at the second Miraval meeting, members of the newly-formed Bravewell Collaborative reconfirmed their commitment to underwrite the costs of its infrastructure and the facilitation of its meetings for the next five years.

"It may sound trivial because the amount of money we gave them wasn't that much," remarks Bill George. "But they had no way of coming together. They had no funding to pay for continued meetings. So in the end, our support made all the difference in the world."

Bravewell would ultimately extend its funding of the Consortium for ten years, for a total of $1.5 million.

CHANGING THE CURRICULUM

In the spirit of "no green bananas," in 2003, Bravewell encouraged the Academic Consortium leadership to make their core competency work available to all medical schools. The leaders accepted the challenge and "Core Competencies in Integrative Medicine for Medical School Curricula: A Proposal," was published in the June 2004 issue of *Academic Medicine*, the official journal of the American Association of Medical Colleges.

A second project—to compile detailed integrative medicine curricula that were being taught at different medical schools across the country—was also undertaken. Edited by Benjamin Kligler, MD, MPH, Rita Benn, PhD, and Gwen Alexander, PhD, members of the Academic Consortium developed a workbook and companion

> ## "CORE COMPETENCIES" AUTHORS
>
> Rita Benn, PhD
>
> Tracy Gaudet, MD
>
> Benjamin Kligler, MD, MPH
>
> Roberta Lee, MD
>
> Victoria Maizes, MD
>
> Constance Park, MD, PhD
>
> Rachel Naomi Remen, MD
>
> Steven Schachter, MD

CD containing examples of integrative medicine curricula. Funded by Bravewell, six hundred copies of *Curriculum in Integrative Medicine: A Guide for Medical Educators* were distributed in May 2004 to deans, associate deans, and medical school faculty throughout the country.

"The effort was very worthwhile," remarks Victoria Maizes, MD, executive director of the Center for Integrative Medicine at the University of Arizona. "The *Curriculum in Integrative Medicine* has been widely used for years."

NEW COMMUNITIES OF PRACTICE

The Consortium soon established working groups in clinical care, education, research, and policy. These *communities of practice* have furthered the advancement and adoption of integrative medicine by developing models of care, facilitating the incorporation of integrative medicine into all levels of medical education, supporting high-quality research, and influencing local, state, and national health policy.

MEMBERSHIP

With the financial support of The Bravewell Collaborative, the academic leaders were able to focus on their work and widening their circles of influence. Universities that might not have otherwise spent a few thousand dollars to send people to a meeting did not object to sending them if the meeting was funded.

The Academic Consortium quickly expanded, growing from eight members to twelve, then to twenty, thirty, and more. In 2015, at the time of this writing, there are sixty-five members, representing more than one third of all US medical schools, several medical schools from Canada and Mexico, and some of the leading health systems in North America.

AN IMPORTANT CONFERENCE

Understanding the value of and need for a growing body of evidence, the Consortium launched its first research conference in 2006. In keeping with the values inherent in integrative medicine, to produce the conference, the Consortium partnered with other organizations, including the International Society for Complementary Medicine Research, the Integrative Health Policy Consortium, and the Academic Consortium for Complementary and Alternative Health Care. Thanks to hard work and careful planning, their congress quickly grew in size and stature and has since become the largest international integrative medicine research conference in the world.

The concentric circles of influence were extending farther than anyone at that initial Fetzer meeting had dreamed.

BRAVEWELL'S CONTRIBUTION

While there were certainly many factors contributing to the rise of integrative medicine and the success of the Academic Consortium, Bravewell's contribution is clear. "The Consortium would not be the strong and vibrant force it is today in the world of integrative health-care were it not for the tremendous support we received over the past ten years from The Bravewell Collaborative," explains Ben Kligler, MD, MPH, previous chair (2012–2013) of the Academic Consortium. "One way to think about Bravewell's impact is to realize that in 2000, only eight medical schools had active integrative medicine programs. By 2015, more than sixty major medical schools and health systems were engaged in research, education, and clinical practice in integrative medicine. As a result, not only did more people have access to clinical services, but because of the research efforts, the evidence base for integrative medicine grew tremendously and medical school curricula simultaneously began to regularly include integrative medicine topics."

"It's very unusual to have such dedicated people who are movers and shakers in their own fields be willing to partner with people who are actually doing the work," adds Brian Berman, MD. "Usually there is a dividing line and a sense of hierarchy between the philanthropists and the people they are funding. But with Bravewell, everyone was willing to work together, to understand what the needs of the field were, and then to launch strategic efforts to move that along."

COMING OF AGE
Part of the success of both Bravewell and the Academic Consortium had to do with building credibility in the places where it counted. "The Academic Consortium was a perfect leverage point, and it was essential to have universities like Harvard and Duke leading the way," explains Diane Neimann.

Everyone understood that the timeline for seeing results from the Consortium's efforts would be longer than some of the other initiatives, but that staying the course was imperative. "In this regard, providing that second round of funding was really as important as providing the first," adds Bill Sarnoff. This funding would provide the time for the Consortium to begin to advance the evidence base, another critical element in building credibility in mainstream medicine. Bravewell members were also well aware that their funding of the Consortium could not be sustained forever. "To a certain extent, if the Consortium never reached the place where it was operating on its own, our strategy would not have been a success," explains Diane.

The philanthropists informed the Consortium, well in advance, that Bravewell funding would be decreasing and then eventually stopping. This gave the Consortium leadership time to develop a plan for sustainability. While philanthropic gifts are still sought, the Consortium's sources of income now include membership dues, grants, sponsorships, and revenues from meetings, among others.

A LEGACY GIFT TO BRAVEWELL

In the fall of 2012, the Academic Consortium for Integrative Medicine & Health announced that it had established two programs to honor the many contributions made by The Bravewell Collaborative to the field of integrative healthcare and to the Consortium.

The Bravewell Lectureship, which is now offered every year at the annual meeting, gives the Consortium the opportunity to invite a thought leader from the larger healthcare world to educate and inspire the membership. The Bravewell Distinguished Service Award is a way of honoring one of the Consortium members for his or her contribution to the Consortium's work.

EMERGENCE

A new system of *influence* that possessed new qualities and generated knowledge did, indeed, emerge as the Academic Consortium came of age.

"Ten years ago we didn't know where the field was headed," explains Adam Perlman, MD, MPH, executive director of Duke Integrative

Medicine and previous chair of the Academic Consortium (2010–2011). "We did not know that the principles of integrative medicine—such as patient-centered care, partnering with patients, considering issues of mind, body, and spirit, and a focus on lifestyle and prevention—would so nicely align with healthcare reform, and that healthcare reform and the Affordable Care Act would lead to a surge of interest in integrative medicine. Ten years ago, we simply believed in what we were doing and forged ahead."

In large part thanks to the Academic Consortium (and thus Bravewell), when interest in these topics swelled, integrative medicine had a decade of academic research and clinical experience under its belt, so that the field could play an important role in the continuing transformation of healthcare in the United States.

> **Health is a state of physical, mental, emotional, and spiritual well-being and not merely the absence of disease.**
> — WORLD HEALTH ORGANIZATION

The true importance of prevention and health were other aspects that emerged from the movement. "One thing that happened in the last ten years is that integrative medicine has focused on health as well as healing," remarks Margaret Chesney, PhD, current chair of the Academic Consortium. "Early programs emphasized treatment of acute issues associated with chronic conditions, such as pain. Now we have a greater focus on prevention and health. This began with the effort to build resilience as part of the healing process and has since grown into the recognition of the importance of disease prevention. In addition, our focus on health and prevention is beginning to reach beyond the clinic into the community. This includes both providing integrative medicine to the underserved and a recognition that there are steps communities can take to promote health."

As time marches forward, more and more Academic Consortium centers are creating community partnerships and reaching out to their communities with programs and events.

"Bravewell always believed that the health of the American people was critical to our nation's economic and competitive future and should be treated as a sustainable resource," notes Christy Mack. "Health is fundamental to everything we do, and it is what enables us to engage with life. For every major decision we face, we should ask: What impact does this decision have on health?"

CONSORTIUM LEADERSHIP

Brian Berman, MD *(Chair 2002–2004)*

Aviad Haramati, PhD *(Vice Chair 2002–2004)*

Susan Folkman, PhD *(Chair 2005–2007)*

Mary Jo Kreitzer, RN, PhD *(Vice Chair 2005–2007)*

Victor Sierpina, MD *(Chair 2008–2009)*

Adam Perlman, MD, MPH, *(Vice Chair 2008–2009, Chair 2010–2011)*

Ben Kligler, MD, MPH *(Vice Chair 2010–2011, Chair 2012–2013)*

Margaret Chesney, PhD *(Vice Chair 2012–2013, Chair 2014–2016)*

Robert Saper, MD *(Vice Chair 2014–2015, Chair 2016–2018)*

CHAPTER SEVEN

Sensemaking

"A map does not just chart, it unlocks
and formulates meaning;
it forms bridges between here and there,
between disparate ideas that we did not know
were previously connected."

— REIF LARSEN

S ENSEMAKING, A TERM FIRST INTRODUCED by organizational theorist Karl Weick, refers to the ability to "structure the unknown so as to be able to act on it." As Deborah Ancona of the MIT Sloan School of Management explains in the *Handbook for Teaching Leadership,* "Sensemaking involves coming up with a plausible understanding—a map—of a shifting world; testing this map with others through data collection, action, and conversation; and then refining, or abandoning, the map depending on how credible it is."

She adds, "Sensemaking enables leaders to have a better grasp of what is going on in their environments, thus facilitating other leadership activities such as visioning, relating, and inventing."

When Bravewell members were first deliberating about how to operationalize their chosen strategies, they realized that in order to make informed decisions, they needed to "make sense of" the current state of integrative medicine in relation to the healthcare environment. In short, they needed a map.

"Integrative medicine was emerging in many forms and in many places," explains Diane Neimann. "It was being shaped by the efforts of clinicians, educators, researchers, and consumers across the country. We knew that if we were going to help this emergence gain traction, we needed a detailed understanding of what was happening and who was making it happen."

Consequently, in 2001, in partnership with Clohesy Consulting, Bravewell undertook a "mapping" (or sensemaking) study that would develop a broad understanding of the forces at work in the emergence of integrative medicine by identifying, documenting, and illuminating the existing landscape of this rapidly developing field. The results of the first project, *Mapping the Emergence of Integrative Medicine*, helped guide Bravewell's work by identifying leaders and other resources in the field as well as the obstacles to moving integrative medicine into mainstream healthcare. It pointed to signs of the cultural shift to integrative medicine and provided important guidance for the establishment of the Bravewell Clinical Network. (See Chapter Eight.)

In 2004, a second phase of the mapping project, *Examples of the Emergence of Integrative Medicine in Communities*, gathered data on how and why integrative approaches gained standing in their respective organizations, which elements of integrative medicine were being applied, and how integration occurred. In 2006, the third phase, *The Effect of Consumer-Directed Health Plans on Access to Integrative Medicine*, examined access to integrative care.

"The value the mapping projects brought to our planning process did not depend on how well the study characterized every form of integrative medicine in every community," remarks Christy Mack, "but rather on how well it signaled important changes and to what degree it helped formulate a context for understanding those changes."

IDENTIFYING THE LEADING MODELS OF CARE

In 2009, conducting another pro bono study for The Bravewell Collaborative, McKinsey & Company analyzed the continued emergence of integrative medicine and how it could best be supported by philanthropy. McKinsey recommended that Bravewell focus on strategies having a national impact, such as conducting large demonstration projects that would document the cost and clinical effectiveness of integrative medicine. As a means of informing these potential research projects, advisor Ralph Snyderman suggested that Bravewell first identify and catalog leading models of integrative care throughout the nation.

Members agreed a new mapping project would be prudent. It could increase awareness of how and where integrative medicine was being practiced, provide much needed information on existing successful models of care, and potentially establish new relationships that might help further Bravewell's strategic goals.

In 2011, Bravewell appointed a Mapping Committee—comprised of Bonnie Horrigan, Connie Pechura, PhD, Donald Abrams, MD, and Sheldon Lewis—to complete the work. The final report, *Integrative Medicine in America: How Integrative Medicine is Being Practiced in Clinical Centers Across the United States*, was released in February 2012. Based on information from 29 of the leading integrative medicine centers, the documentation: (1) described the patient populations and diseases most commonly treated, (2) defined the core practices and models of care, (3) reviewed relevant outcomes data, (4) clarified how the care was paid for, and (5) identified the biggest factors driving successful implementation.

In March 2012, The Bravewell Collaborative invited the leaders of the participating centers to join Bravewell Collaborative members for a one-day meeting in Washington, DC, to discuss the report and deliberate on how to further advance integrative medicine.

A VISION ARISES FROM THE BRAINSTORMING

One of the observations that kept arising in conversations during this meeting was that while there were many places to receive clinical training, there wasn't anywhere a person could go to learn how to establish an integrative medicine program or how to successfully expand one that was already in place. As the participants in the room recounted obstacles to expansion, it became obvious that it was going to take more than clinical skills to bring integrative medicine into the mainstream. Leadership was needed.

After listening carefully to these comments, Bravewell members agreed to investigate the idea of creating a leadership program that would address this need. (See Chapter Seventeen.)

"One of Bravewell's strengths was our ability to convene, our ability to bring the right people together and to facilitate a meaningful, productive conversation," explains Ann Lovell. "That's what happened with the mapping convening. And out of it came the idea for a whole new program that is now, today, training integrative medicine leaders from across the country. Witness the power of honoring the wisdom of the group."

CHAPTER EIGHT

Creating Models for Change

~~~

*"You never change things by fighting the existing realty.
To change something, build a new model that
makes the existing model obsolete."*

— R. BUCKMINSTER FULLER

ANOTHER *COMMUNITY OF PRACTICE* that emerged from Bravewell's work was the Bravewell Clinical Network.

The concept of "communities of practice" was first articulated by Jean Lave and Etienne Wegner in their book, *Situated Learning: Legitimate Peripheral Participation*. According to Wegner, "communities of practice are formed by people who engage in a process of collective learning in a shared domain of human endeavor: a tribe learning to survive, a band of artists seeking new forms of expression, a group of engineers working on similar problems...." These communities can evolve organically because people share a common interest, or they can be deliberately created with the goal of advancing the members' knowledge base. Wegner goes on to explain that through the process of sharing information with one another, members of the community expand their own knowledge base. Everyone is elevated.

The Bravewell Clinical Network was an intentionally created community of practice.

ESTABLISHING THE NETWORK

At both the Miraval and Pocantico meetings, the philanthropists deliberated over which strategies would provide the most leverage in moving integrative medicine forward. During those conversations, they quickly realized that it would be essential to have examples of what success actually looked like. In short, they needed to be able to point to integrative medicine centers that were not only delivering outstanding care but were also financially viable.

"The real test and benefit of any medicine is in the care of patients in clinical practice," explains Diane Neimann. "We needed to be able to show, without reservation, that not only did integrative medicine work, but it was also replicable and sustainable across a variety of healthcare settings."

Initially, there were only a handful of integrative medicine centers leading the way, and most of those were struggling financially. However, the philanthropists felt that simply infusing cash into these centers was not a sustainable solution. They looked at the problem through an old but trusted principle—*Give a man a fish and you feed him for a day. Teach him to fish and you feed him for a lifetime.*

In 2002, before setting their strategic course, at Bravewell's request, McKinsey & Company conducted a $1 million pro bono management study of six of the leading integrative medicine centers.

While McKinsey offered a number of recommendations for overcoming the barriers to success, the study strongly recommended that Bravewell develop a network (*a community of practice*) among the leading centers, so they could share lessons learned, help each other build clinical capacity, and develop viable business models.

Offering another perspective, Bill George explains that, "Harvard Business School professor Michael Porter, PhD, MBA, talks about the value of clusters, which are geographic concentrations of companies, suppliers, service providers, or associated institutions in a particular field. Their proximity to each other increases productivity. You see it in New York City around art and in Silicon Valley around computers. It's about very creative people feeding off each other's ideas."

"Our challenge was that the most creative people in the field of integrative medicine were spread all around the country—even all around the world," he adds. "So we needed to bring them together; we needed to create a virtual cluster."

In 2003, the Bravewell membership fully embraced the idea of creating a "Clinical Network" that would build community and facilitate the exchange of information. As with the Academic Consortium, the members agreed to fund the chosen centers' participation for the in-person gatherings, and once again, this foundational support made all the difference in the world.

Members of the Bravewell Clinical Network held their first meeting at the Pocantico Conference Center of the Rockefeller Brothers Fund in January 2004, and continued to meet twice a year until Bravewell's closing.

"You have to realize that what Bravewell did, we never did ourselves. We simply provided structure, stability, and funding for the people who were already involved," remarks Ann Lovell. "Our work was leveraging others, facilitating, and bringing people to the table. This can be a huge gift, because what comes from those meetings, what comes from connecting people, can be life-changing, and often world-changing."

A RISING TIDE FLOATS ALL BOATS

Mimi Guarneri, MD, had worked closely with Diane Neimann and Penny George to help plan the first Miraval event and visualize how integrative medicine could be moved into the mainstream. She had also co-founded, with Rauni King, RN, a successful integrative medicine center at Scripps Health in La Jolla, California, which in 2002 was one of the few viable centers in the country. So when the Clinical Network was being established, The Bravewell Board of Directors asked Mimi if she would be its chair.

She said yes. "The goal was to have a network of clinical sites that would work together. Usually everyone's in competition with one another, but from what I knew of the field, I thought we could do it," explains Mimi. "The mainstream medical movement did not understand what we were doing, nor did they understand that they were focused on disease care while we were focused on prevention and chronic disease management and delivering compassionate, holistic care. And they weren't going to understand it unless they could see it. So we all knew that the success of one center was really the success of all the centers."

CREATING COMMUNITY

Charles Terry facilitated the Clinical Network meetings, which he did

> Mimi Guarneri, MD, chaired the Clinical Network from 2004 to mid-2012.
>
> Donald Abrams, MD, chaired the Clinical Network from mid-2012 to June 2015.

with his usual focus on fostering a deeper human connection among the people in the room. "I have been involved in starting a number of organizations, some of which really flourished," explains Charles. "So I've seen it over and over. Money and knowledge are helpful, but when you bring people together on a deeper level, it makes a huge difference."

One of the tools of the trade Charles used was to hold opening and closing circles in which everyone was asked to speak briefly on a certain subject such as, what is new in your life or what challenge are you currently facing? "Just making room for everybody to think about and communicate whatever they are feeling is a powerful tool," he explains.

Of course, not everyone was smitten with this type of sharing as Myles Spar, MD, MPH, director of integrative medicine at the Simms/Mann Health and Wellness Center at Venice Family Clinic quickly found out. "When I first invited our program manager to come to a Clinical Network meeting, I thought she was going to stand up and walk out of the room during the first opening circle," Myles laughs. "But it wasn't too long before she was looking forward to the circles as much as to the data-focused parts of the meeting."

"There were both practical and tangible aspects, and then there was the intangible, which for me, was the most valuable," says Tracy Gaudet, MD, former director of Duke Integrative Medicine and current director of the Office of Patient-Centered Care and Cultural Transformation for the Veterans Health Administration. "In those early days, it was like warfare. Every day you were fighting the system over this or that, and it was exhausting. So the sustenance—just that caring, the support, and knowing that someone believed in us—is what kept us going."

DIVERSITY OF MEMBERSHIP

The centers that comprised the clinical network were chosen, in part, because they represented some of the best integrative practices in the United States. But Bravewell also ensured that different models were represented. Members of the network included:

❋ Clinics operated by three large health systems
(Scripps Health in California, Allina Health in Minnesota, and Beth Israel Medical Center in New York)

❋ A stand-alone clinic owned by its physicians
(Alliance in Ohio)

❋ Clinics established within four university medical school systems
(Duke University in North Carolina, University of California, San Francisco, University of Maryland, and Jefferson University in Pennsylvania)

❋ A clinic established by a physician's group
(Northwestern in Illinois)

❋ A center run by a free clinic
(Venice Family Clinic in California)

"We needed the Clinical Network to have enough diversity so that the models of care were relevant to a continuum of possibilities within healthcare," explains Christy Mack.

Having a free clinic in the network was an important statement. "Being a member of the Bravewell Clinical Network has brought those without financial means and with poor access to healthcare to the table. The importance of this cannot be overstated," explains Myles. "In inviting Venice Family Clinic to join the network, Bravewell showed that it stood for integrative medicine as a solution to the problem of access to good healthcare in the United States. It showed Bravewell's commitment to demonstrating that integrative medicine can be used to prevent some of the health challenges that disproportionately affect those with lower incomes and poor access to care, and it showed that integrative medicine is the solution to the many problems faced by our nation's healthcare system."

BUSINESS PLANNING

At the time of the Clinical Network's formation, most of the centers were operating at a loss. Based on the recommendations from McKinsey & Company's pro bono study that each center create a business plan, Bravewell hired Susan Stock of Neela Associates, Inc. to work with the Clinical Network members, guiding them in the process of developing their own business plan based on their unique circumstances. With its own plan, each center would then be able to address marketing strategies, practice implementations, and financial management so that it would be better equipped to achieve viability.

"This process helped the centers move toward sustainability and gain firmer footing within their own institutions. It also serves as a perfect example of our funding of the overall vision for integrative medicine," remarks Christy.

STAYING CONNECTED WITH THE WORK

As with all of Bravewell's initiatives, the Clinical Network was fully staffed from the onset. In addition, members of the Bravewell Board of Directors regularly attended the meetings so they could observe progress and be kept informed about the work being done by these integrative leaders.

MILESTONES

In addition to business planning and the sharing of information at the meetings, the members of the Clinical Network participated in other Bravewell programs:

✴ The Bravewell Fellowship Program, which trained physicians to be integrative medicine specialists (see Chapter Nine), was adopted at the second meeting in July 2004 in La Jolla, California.

✴ In the fall of 2007, with Bravewell's financial support, the Clinical Network members published the highly consulted *Best Practices in Integrative Medicine: A Report from the Bravewell Clinical Network*.

✴ In 2008, with financial assistance from The Bravewell Collaborative and advice from the National Cancer Institute (NCI) and the Office of the Director at the National Institutes of Health (NIH), the Clinical Network organized BraveNet, the first practice-based research network (PBRN) in integrative medicine. (See Chapter Sixteen.)

THE CREATION OF VALUE

One lesson learned from the centers that opened in the 1980s and early 1990s, many of which were set up to compete with the existing healthcare system and many of which have since closed or reorganized, was that the public did not want to choose between conventional and integrative medicine—for the most part, they wanted both. When center leadership changed the way they approached their own institutions and the healthcare system at large, integrative medicine began to flourish.

A good example is what Jon Kabat-Zinn accomplished with mindfulness. Aware that many healthcare practitioners and systems objected to meditation as an intervention because they felt it promoted Buddhism, Jon abstracted the basic process and renamed it Mindfulness-Based Stress Reduction, which removed it from religious connotations and tied it to a health issue. Then, instead of confining mindfulness to patient care, it was also offered as an answer to challenges any organization might face, such as physician burnout or faculty resiliency. Thus, mindfulness came to be seen as a solution to widespread problems rather than an isolated integrative intervention. Recognizing win-win opportunities such as this—looking for ways to helpfully situate oneself within the current culture or solve a larger institutional challenge rather than being dogmatic in one's approach and remaining outside the culture—creates the means for greater acceptance and eventual transformation.

"The question to answer is this: Where can the principles and practices of integrative healthcare bring added value to the organization?" explains Adam Perlman, MD, MPH, executive director of Duke Integrative Medicine.

Members of the Clinical Network embraced this approach—building alliances and creating win-win situations—early on. For example, the Osher Center for Integrative Medicine at the University of California, San Francisco (UCSF) works closely with the UCSF Helen Diller Family Comprehensive Cancer Center to support people with cancer on their journey. Patients find the addition of integrative care to the regimen helps with both recovery and survivorship, which the conventional oncologists also value, and over the years, referrals to the Osher Center from the UCSF Cancer Center have tripled.

During the past decade, the Penny George Institute for Health and Healing at Abbott Northwestern Hospital expanded its reach by offering inpatient services to support the healing process for hospitalized patients. "The program has proven so successful in reducing pain, anxiety, and nausea that Allina Health is instituting it in its ten other Allina hospitals," explains Courtney Baechler, MD, vice president of the Penny George Institute.

Collaboration and integration have proven to be key factors to growth. "One of the things we are most pleased with is our ability to build bridges to other departments in our own health system and achieve a high level of service line integration, so that integrative medicine isn't this department off in the corner but is a thriving integral part of what the whole institution does," says Daniel Monti, MD, executive director of the Jefferson–Myrna Brind Center of Integrative Medicine. "We have numerous collaborative clinical protocols with the Cancer Center and several joint initiatives with the hospital for employee wellness. Our faculty frequently present lectures in departments throughout the hospital and university campus, and our CME-approved Integrative Medicine Grand Rounds is frequently attended by faculty in other departments."

In addition to establishing a partnership with the R Adams Cowley Shock Trauma Center, the Center for Integrative Medicine at the University of Maryland collaborates on research projects and education. "We are part of the culture now," says Brian Berman, MD, director of the Center for Integrative Medicine. "We have a seat at the roundtable."

AN ENDURING COMMUNITY

As the Bravewell Clinical Network built a *community of practice*, it also built an enduring community among its members. "Being in the Clinical Network made us feel like we were part of a bigger picture," remarks Sandi Amoils, MD, co-director of the Alliance Center for Integrative Medicine. "It wasn't that we were just this one little center in the middle of the country trying to do something. We realized it was a national movement and we were part of it. That helped to keep us inspired."

The exposure to the ideas and practices of other leading centers resulted in cross-fertilization. "We all have our own lens through which we see the world, but when we can collaborate in the way the Bravewell Clinical Network has allowed us to, then you see things that you wouldn't see otherwise, and many things become possible that wouldn't have been possible before," adds Tracy.

"It was invaluable to be able to share what worked and what didn't work, to be able to help each other and not have to reinvent the wheel every time you wanted to do something," explains Mimi. "We created a network of colleagues, which we will forever have in our lives, people who have become friends and whom we can call at the drop of a hat. The Bravewell Clinical Network was a unique and powerful experience."

CLINICAL NETWORK MEMBER CENTERS

At the time of Bravewell's closing, the Clinical Network had fourteen member centers.

Alliance Institute for Integrative Medicine
Cincinnati, Ohio
> *Steve Amoils, MD, Founder and Director*
> *Sandi Amoils, MD, Founder and Director*

Boston Medical Center, Boston University
Boston, Massachusetts
> *Robert Saper, MD, MPH, Director*
> *Paula Gardiner, MD, Assistant Director*

Integrative Medicine at the University of Colorado, Denver
Denver, Colorado
> *Lisa Corbin, MD, Medical Director*
> *Jacinda Nicklas, MD, MPH, MA, Assistant Professor*

Mount Sinai Beth Israel Center for Health and Healing
New York, New York
> *Woodson Merrell, MD, Executive Director*
> *Benjamin Kligler, MD, MPH, Vice Chair and Research Director*
> *Roberta Lee, MD, former Medical Director*

Duke Integrative Medicine, Duke University
Durham, North Carolina
> *Adam Perlman, MD, Executive Director*
> *Ruth Wolever, PhD, former Research Director*
> *Tracy Gaudet, MD, former and Founding Director*

Jefferson–Myrna Brind Center of Integrative Medicine at Thomas
> Jefferson Medical College
Philadelphia, Pennsylvania
> *Daniel Monti, MD, Executive Director*
> *Andrew Newberg, MD, Director of Research*
> *Joel Edman, DSc, former Director of Integrative Nutrition*

Center for Integrative Medicine at the University of Maryland
    School of Medicine
Baltimore, Maryland
Brian Berman, MD, Director
Chris D'Adamo, PhD, Director of Research
William Rollow, MD, MPH, Director of Clinical Services
Joyce Frye, DO, MBA, former Integrative Family Physician
Elizabeth Kimbrough Pradhan, MPH, PhD, former Assistant
    Professor

Osher Center for Integrative Medicine at Northwestern University
Chicago, Illinois
Melinda Ring, MD, Medical Director
David Victorson, MD, Associate Professor

Osher Center for Integrative Medicine at the University of
    California, San Francisco
San Francisco, California
Margaret Chesney, PhD, Executive Director
Donald Abrams, MD, Integrative Oncology Research
Susan Folkman, PhD, former Director
Kevin Barrows, MD, former Director of Clinical Programs

Penny George Institute for Health and Healing Abbott
    Northwestern Hospital
Minneapolis, Minnesota
Courtney Baechler, MD, MS, Vice President Clinical Service Line
Jeffery Dusek, PhD, Research Director
Lori Knutson, RN, BSN, former Director

University of Pittsburgh Center for Integrative Medicine
Pittsburgh, Pennsylvania
Neil Ryan, MD, Director
Carol Greco, PhD, Assistant Professor

Scripps Center for Integrative Medicine
La Jolla, California
 Chris Suhar, MD, Medical Director
 Mimi Guarneri, MD, Founder and former Medical Director
 Rauni King, RN, Founder and former Director of Programs and
  Planning

Simms/Mann Health and Wellness Center at the Venice
 Family Clinic
Los Angeles, California
 Myles Spar, MD, Director of Integrative Medicine
 Nancy Rodriguez, MPH, former Clinical Program Manager

The Osher Center for Integrative Health at Vanderbilt University
Nashville, Tennessee
 Roy Elam, MD, Medical Director
 Gurjeet Birdee, MD, Director of Research

PRIOR MEMBER CENTERS

Advocate Center for Complementary Medicine (2005–2007)
Chicago, Illinois

Canadian Institute of Natural and Integrative Medicine
 (2004–2005)
Calgary, Alberta, Canada

CHAPTER NINE

Increasing Capacity

❧

*"Education is the most powerful weapon
which you can use to change the world."*

— NELSON MANDELA

"**C**ORE COMPETENCY" IS A CONCEPT identified by C.K. Prahalad and Gary Hamel in an article that originally appeared in the May 1990 issue of the *Harvard Business Review.* They defined a core competency as a specific factor that a business or professional discipline sees as being central or critical to the way it works. Core competencies can take various forms, including technical subject matter and know-how, reliable processes and procedures, the approach to relationships, and the embodiment of specific cultural tenets.

Although people have been training others in fundamental skill sets for thousands of years, naming and elucidating the process helped more-recent leaders understand the value of identifying and teaching those competencies needed to accomplish certain undertakings specific to their industry. Within medicine, the fellowship model is broadly used to teach physicians the knowledge and skills needed to practice a certain medical specialty such as cardiology, hematology, or immunology. Creating a fellowship program that trained practitioners in the core competencies of integrative medicine would prove to be an important factor in the overall growth and acceptance of this field.

THE FELLOWSHIP

In 1994, Andrew Weil, MD, founded the Center for Integrative Medicine at the University of Arizona in Tucson, Arizona. "My interest and vision was to transform medical practice and healthcare," he explains. "I thought the best way to do that would be by focusing on the medical education and training of a new generation of physicians and allied health professionals who would understand the body's natural healing mechanisms and the role of mind, body, and spirit in health, and who would be open to using a wide variety of treatments."

Together with his team, he launched the Residential Fellowship in Integrative Medicine in 1997. A large part of the creation process involved identifying the core competencies needed to practice integrative medicine.

By 2000, the Fellowship in Integrative Medicine had evolved to become the two-year, distance-learning (online) program it is today. While most of the study is completed off-site, three residential weeks in Tucson, Arizona, foster personal growth and community building.

"Participating in the Fellowship re-energizes, restructures, and reframes a person's perspective of medicine. It teaches a new way of caring for patients, with emphasis on the individual, not simply the disease, and on prevention, not just treatment," explains Victoria Maizes, MD, the executive director of the Arizona Center for Integrative Medicine.

THE CORE COMPETENCIES TAUGHT BY THE FELLOWSHIP IN INTEGRATIVE MEDICINE AT THE UNIVERSITY OF ARIZONA INCLUDE:

✳ Providing healthcare services aimed at preventing illness and promoting health and wellness

✳ In-depth understanding and application of nutrition in healthcare

✳ Mastery of the evidence base of research as it pertains to dietary supplements, including dosing, appropriate use, potential side effects, and supplement–drug interactions

✳ Understanding of the foundations and applications of mind-body medicine and spirituality in practice

✳ Foundations of well-being including a solid foundation of self-care, physical activity, sleep, and elements of mental heath such as resilience, compassion, and optimism

✳ Understanding of the scope and history of selected whole medical systems including traditional Chinese medicine, Ayurveda, and naturopathy, and how their roots inform elements of modern integrative medicine practice

✳ Grasp of the medical-legal issues involved in the safe and ethical practice of integrative medicine

✳ Development of integrative approaches to a range of common medical conditions in rheumatology, cardiovascular disease, women's health, men's health, chronic pain, diabetes, gastrointestinal disease, respiratory conditions, oncology, neurologic conditions, and pediatrics

✳ Familiarity with the evolving research base in the human biofield and energy medicine

✳ Understanding of the influence of environmental health on human health.

THE BRAVEWELL CONNECTION: IDENTIFYING THE NEED FOR INCREASED CAPACITY

Colby and Alana (Lani) Jones became interested in integrative medicine after Lani was diagnosed with rheumatoid arthritis. Dissatisfaction with the mainstream perspective led them to search for a more integrative approach. After moving to Tucson for a short period for Colby's business interests, Colby connected with Andy Weil. "He used to have one-week seminars in remote places. I attended one, and it was one of the better experiences of my life," Colby remarks. "At the end of the program, Andy explained that he was trying to put together a program to educate doctors in integrative medicine. He asked if anybody would be interested to help financially, and that's how our relationship started."

Colby helped fund the launch of the Fellowship Program, and it was during this time that he met Lu Lovell, who was also supporting the Fellowship program. When she returned from Bravewell's Pocantico meeting, Lu asked Colby to join Bravewell. Colby declined. "After reviewing who was participating, I told Lu that in my judgment there were too many egos in pursuit of their own goals for the group to be able to agree on a master plan," Colby explains.

A year later, after watching Bravewell coalesce and a master plan emerge, he changed his mind and joined. "What can I say?" he laughs. "I was wrong."

Like many Bravewell members who had strong business backgrounds, Colby was well aware that *consumer demand for integrative medicine was growing faster than the system's capacity to deliver it.* At the spring meeting in 2003, Colby suggested that expanding the University of Arizona's Fellowship in Integrative Medicine program might be an effective way to increase delivery capacity while at the same time holding true to Bravewell's values of (1) not reinventing the wheel and (2) partnering with the people who were already doing the work. His idea was to offer full "Bravewell" scholarships for the Fellowship to a certain number of physicians, physician assistants, and nurse practitioners each year.

However, as originally conceived by the University of Arizona, the Fellowship did not offer any clinical experience, and Bravewell members believed that clinical practice under the guidance of a mentor was essential. So after discussing Colby's proposition, they devised an expanded format for the "Bravewell Fellowship" that would include a supervised clinical experience at the centers in the Bravewell Clinical Network.

After the Bravewell Board of Directors fully embraced this idea as a strategy for training more clinicians in integrative medicine and making the "new medicine" accessible to more people, Colby and Lani Jones pledged $1 million in the form of a challenge grant. It was soon matched by other Bravewell members.

ECHOING THE NEED

Sherry Lund was one of the board members who lent their full support to Colby's suggestion. Friends for many years, Penny George introduced Sherry to Bravewell. "The whole idea appealed to me," explains Sherry. After meeting Diane Neimann and talking further, Sherry joined Bravewell in 2005. "What spoke to me right away was the Fellowship, because I was very adamant that we needed more trained doctors who could actually deliver integrative medicine."

A big part of Sherry's desire to see integrative medicine grow stemmed from the death of her sister from leukemia in 1978. Her doctor had been smart enough to recognize that Sherry's sister needed emotional support, and so guided imagery and expressive art were part of her therapy. "Those things really helped her," Sherry adds.

REFINING THE CONCEPT

The concept for the Bravewell Fellowship was presented to the

Clinical Network during its meeting in January 2004. Making a commitment to the pilot project meant that each center would recruit several Bravewell Fellowship candidates consistent with University of Arizona requirements and, during the course of their training, provide them with a supervised clinical experience. It meant that already busy people would be taking on extra work for which there was no personal financial incentive. True to the nature of the people involved, the members of the Clinical Network unanimously agreed to participate in the pilot because they knew it was important to their vision and would benefit the whole field. The Bravewell Collaborative pledged to underwrite the tuition and travel expenses for the people chosen to become Bravewell Fellows.

Following this commitment, Andrew Weil, MD, Victoria Maizes, MD, and others from the Center for Integrative Medicine at the University of Arizona worked with The Bravewell Collaborative and the Clinical Network to fully develop the unique Bravewell Fellowship so that the program would not only provide clinical experience, but also create a strong community of leaders in integrative medicine.

THE BRAVEWELL FELLOWSHIP

The pilot phase of the Bravewell Fellowship began in January 2005. Bravewell awarded twenty-four full scholarships and four partial scholarships to physicians and nurse practitioners chosen by the members of the Clinical Network.

As the first class of Fellows was approaching graduation (December 2006), Bravewell members conducted an evaluation of the pilot program to assess its effectiveness. The reviews were extremely positive, and after learning that the Fellowship had, in fact, made a significant difference in how the Fellows practiced medicine as well as exerting a positive impact on their personal lives, Bravewell decided to continue funding the program.

"We needed a new generation of physicians," explains Penny George, "and the Fellowship was delivering just that."

The second class of Bravewell Fellows graduated in December 2008. Bravewell was interested in expanding care to the underserved, so in addition to those Fellows connected with the Clinical Network sites, this class included Fellows from the community-based clinics at the University of California, Los Angeles, the University of California, San Diego, and the NIH Clinical Center in Bethesda, Maryland.

By the time this second class graduated and started working in different healthcare settings across the country, the effect of the program was noticeable, as the Fellows took leadership positions in major medical centers such as Duke, the University of Miami, the Mayo Clinic, and Johns Hopkins. According to Lu Lovell, "The ripple effect from the training of doctors was immeasurable. The Fellows were excited, and they were telling other people about their experiences and about integrative medicine, and those people were telling other people."

The third class, which graduated in December 2010, included two post-doctoral fellows from the National Institute of Nursing Research (NINR) at the National Institutes of Health. The members of the fourth and final class graduated in December 2012.

All told, the Bravewell Fellowship supported and graduated eighty-nine Fellows.

RIPPLE EFFECTS

Each graduate became a nexus for change. Bravewell Fellows now teach in medical schools, run clinical programs, head up research programs, and sit on different committees within a healthcare or academic system. They have multiple opportunities to influence the way healthcare is delivered.

In addition, the Bravewell Fellowship had other ripple effects. "It stimulated us to think further about other kinds of scholarships," explains Victoria. "Because of Bravewell, we created a scholarship for the underserved—for people working at community health centers, federally qualified health centers, and at Indian Health Services. We also provided an academic faculty scholarship."

LONG-TERM RESULTS

"The Bravewell Fellowship is a good example of the strategic way Bravewell chose and then operationalized its initiatives," remarks Ann Lovell. "It addressed and identified needs and supported the people who were already involved in this work. It was designed to further the vision and was something that we could accomplish within a relatively short period of time. And the results speak for themselves."

The Fellowship in Integrative Medicine, which has now graduated more than 1000 fellows, is widely recognized as the leading integrative medical education program in the world. Since its inception, the fellows have applied integrative techniques to more than thirty-five medical specialties, including family practice, cardiology, oncology, pediatrics, OB-GYN, and rheumatology.

"I think one of the best initiatives Bravewell launched was the Fellowship," adds Mimi Guarneri. "The philanthropists recognized that if we didn't have physicians who knew how to practice integrative medicine, the transformation of healthcare would not occur. By training physicians through the University of Arizona's Fellowship program, we now have a network of trained fellows who can lead integrative centers and offer quality care to their patients. That is an incredibly valuable piece of the puzzle."

CHAPTER TEN

Honoring Spirit, Courage, and Vision

"Vision without action is merely a dream.
Action without vision just passes the time.
Vision with action can change the world."

— **JOEL ARTHUR BARKER**

ANY SUCCESSFUL SOCIAL TRANSFORMATION requires champions who not only hold the vision but are also willing to undertake the risks and sacrifices necessary to catalyze change. It is often a lonely job without many social rewards. While recognition often comes late, nearly every organization in every field establishes some sort of award for those who lead the way.

Identifying and supporting the leadership within integrative medicine would prove to be a successful Bravewell strategy, not only for the leaders honored, but also for the field as a whole.

GOOD ADVICE

In 2001, because of her extensive work in both philanthropy and medicine, and in particular on The Project on Death in America, Diane Neimann asked Kathleen Foley, MD, to become a Bravewell advisor. Kathy agreed to help. "In a way, what Bravewell was trying to do had many of the same components as The Project on Death in America. It was philanthropically driven, and there was a need to build the field and to professionalize and expand it," she explains.

At the spring meeting in 2002, Kathy suggested that Bravewell think about a program that would recognize the leaders in the field of integrative medicine. "One of the key elements of our project was that we supported faculty scholars and leaders," she remarks. "The construct was that if one is to build a field within medicine, then you need champions, and *the best strategy is to invest in the leaders who can move the field forward.*"

In due course, Bravewell members developed the Bravewell Leadership Award program to encourage and sustain leadership in the field as well as call attention to integrative medicine's progress and achievements.

THE LEADERSHIP AWARD

Bravewell determined that recipients of the leadership award should be those change agents who had the greatest potential for influencing their peers and institutions, and who possessed the best opportunity to effect long-term change. In setting the criteria for eligibility, Bravewell decided that the candidates needed to be physicians or other doctoral level professionals from North America who:

✳   Were catalysts in advancing the field of integrative medicine

✳   Had made significant contributions to the field of medicine and demonstrated positive influence among their colleagues and those they serve

✳   Embodied and advanced the principles of the Declaration for a New Medicine

✳   Had a history of collaboration across disciplines and healing philosophies

✳   Had a compelling vision for the future of medicine that inspired and encouraged others

✳   Were resilient change agents and role models in their communities.

Five Leadership Awards were bestowed during Bravewell's existence, each one conferring $100,000 to the recipient for advancing his or her work in the field of integrative medicine. Six leaders received a special Pioneer Award that conferred $25,000. All the awardees also received a beautiful, one-of-a-kind glass sphere, created specifically for Bravewell.

"We wanted the award to take the recipients to a place of focus and inspiration that would energize them to continue the good work," explains previous Bravewell member Lynn Getz, who was instrumental in designing the award. "We chose the sphere because it is a universal symbol for humanity. It was weighted at seven pounds because that is the average weight of a newborn, and thus it would symbolize birth. And finally, air bubbles were blown into the clear glass, which then likened the sphere to the universe. Everyone is touched when they look up at the night sky and, metaphorically, that's what we wanted this award to generate—universal connection."

THE AWARD EVENTS

The inaugural Bravewell Leadership Award Event was held on November 13, 2003, in New York City. Ralph Snyderman, MD, former chancellor for health affairs, Duke University Medical Center, and former president and CEO, Duke University Health Systems, accepted the award from Walter Cronkite.

The second Bravewell Leadership Award Event was held on November 10, 2005, in New York City. Brian Berman, MD, director of the Center for Integrative Medicine at the University of Maryland School of Medicine, accepted the award from the Duchess of York, Sarah Ferguson.

"Back in 2005, holding the Leadership Award in my hands, its glass globe conjured a vision of a future with infinite possibility for a better healthcare system, and its bubbles a recognition of the work of the numerous pioneers, past, present, and future, who are transforming the face of medicine," says Brian. "I was very much aware that its significance was larger than me—it came at a time when all of us involved with integrative medicine had many achievements to celebrate and much work still to do."

On November 8, 2007, Bravewell altered its agenda to honor six of integrative medicine's earliest pioneers—Larry Dossey, MD; James Gordon, MD; Jon Kabat-Zinn, PhD; Rachel Remen, MD; Dean Ornish, MD; and Andrew Weil, MD—at the inaugural Bravewell Pioneers of Integrative Medicine Award Event in New York City. To make the most of the Pioneer's extensive knowledge and inspirational presence, Bravewell members added a new component to the Award Dinner—a daytime "Lectures & Luncheon" event, during which each of the Pioneers spoke. The Lectures & Luncheon was open to anyone who wanted to attend and proved to be a resounding success.

"At some stage of their career, all the recipients of the Bravewell Pioneer Awards have known obscurity and the struggles that attend it. While all of them found their voice and achieved notice before receiving the Pioneer Award, the award honored their courage in showing the way," explains Larry Dossey. "The Pioneer Award says, 'You are not alone. Let us help.' I can attest that it is deeply satisfying to be a recipient, and that public approval spurs anyone to greater effort."

With the advent of the Institute of Medicine's Summit on Integrative Medicine and the Health of the Public, the Leadership Award Event for 2009 was postponed as Bravewell focused on a formal dinner event held on November 4, 2009 in Washington, DC, to mark the release of the official *Summary of the Summit*. (See Chapter Thirteen.)

The third Bravewell Leadership Award Event—which honored Mimi Guarneri, MD, founder and director of the Scripps Center for Integrative Medicine—was held on November 10, 2011, in New York City. Mehmet Oz, MD, served as the master of ceremonies. Jon LaPook, MD, CBS Evening News correspondent, moderated the daytime Lectures & Luncheon, which focused on "Integrative

Medicine in Action" within the Department of Defense, Veterans Health Administration, and major US healthcare systems.

On November 7, 2013, in New York City, Bravewell conferred its final leadership awards to Tracy Gaudet, MD, director, VHA Office of Patient-Centered Care and Cultural Transformation, and Myles Spar, MD, director, Integrative Medicine at Venice Family Clinic's Simms/Mann Health and Wellness Center. Mehmet Oz, MD, presided as master of ceremonies, and Harvey Fineberg, MD, MPH, then-president of the Institute of Medicine, delivered the keynote presentation. The final Lectures & Luncheon—Health and Well-being: Integrative Medicine and the Transformation of Healthcare—was moderated once again by Jon LaPook, MD.

FRIEND-RAISERS, NOT FUNDRAISERS

The award events were not billed as fundraising galas. "The reason we were doing these dinners was to create a sense of community among all the providers around the country who felt they were alone," explains Christy Mack. "We wanted people to know that if they came, they were coming because they were a friend and a supporter and a participant in this new vision. It wasn't about dollars."

Hence, the Bravewell dinners were "friend-raisers" instead of fundraisers, she says.

"One thing I loved was that when an event was over, no one wanted to leave," adds Christy. "Usually at a gala, people can't wait to get out the door, but at our dinners everybody would stay and talk to each other. This happened time after time. And without fail, we received comments that people had never been to an award dinner like ours before—ours was fun and intimate."

A GREAT SPEECH BY A GREAT MAN

At the final Bravewell Leadership Award Event, in his keynote address,

Harvey Fineberg, MD, PhD, said, "If you look in your program book, you will find one of Bravewell's important contributions, which is a Patient's Bill of Rights. And if you look over that bill of rights, you will see that it starts out by stating that everyone has a right to person-centered care. It describes the right you have as an individual to truly integrative care, and it concludes by stating that you have a right to be whole. Now, underlying all of these separate rights, is a fundamental right that every individual has to health and healthcare."

He went on to say that, "But in the United States our constitution does not contain any social or economic rights. It remains for us as citizens to assert, to affirm, and to work toward the realization of the right to healthcare for everyone in the United States and, indeed, the right to health for everyone in the world. The rights to health will not occur on their own. They will only arrive when the citizenry decide that it is something we collectively choose to assure."

After tracing the history of social rights in the US, Harvey concluded by saying, "That's why what Bravewell accomplished is so fundamentally important because the whole Bravewell concept is premised on the idea that every person really matters—*that every person has the right to whole care for their whole person.*

"Things change and can change, but they change only because of people like those of you in this room," he concluded. "Only because of the leadership of Bravewell. Only because of people like Penny and Bill George and Christy and John Mack and all of you who have devoted your energy and your resources and your commitments to making health a reality as a right for everyone."

THE PATIENT'S BILL OF RIGHTS

As an individual, you have:

✳ The right to person-centered care.

✳ The right to receive healthcare that addresses the wholeness of who you are—body, mind, and spirit in the context of community.

✳ The right to a healthcare system that focuses on prevention and wellness.

✳ The right to be empowered as the responsible, central actor in your own healing.

✳ The right to education about self-care that includes access to scientifically-based nutrition, exercise, and mind-body interventions.

✳ The right to a healing relationship with your healthcare provider that is grounded in humanism, compassion, and caring.

✳ The right to speak openly and honestly with your healthcare providers and in return, to experience honest and supportive communications from all members of the healthcare community.

✳ The right to a healthcare environment that recognizes that to be healing and empowering, healthcare providers themselves must seek to be restored and whole.

✳ The right to embrace the spiritual dimension in the context of your healthcare.

✳ The right to healthcare providers who understand that integrity and spiritual qualities are as important as medical knowledge and technical skills in the process of healing.

✳ The right to a truly integrative medicine that is supported by rigorous scientific research, maintains the highest standards of excellence, and offers a full and complete array of care modalities.

✳ The right to healing even when there is no cure.

✳ The right to be whole.

IN RETROSPECT

"Like so many things Bravewell did, the Leadership Award program was strategic," adds Tracy Gaudet, MD. "It raised the level of awareness of, and gave a visibility and significance to, the work. What I didn't expect, and what I think was so powerful, was the ripple effect for the field. Having Walter Cronkite confer an award, having Jon LaPook moderate the lectures, having HRH Prince Charles send a video to be shown, having Mehmet Oz be the master of ceremonies, having Harvey Fineberg give a keynote—it took it out of our internal community and acknowledged that a) this is an important movement and important work and b) those leading it should be honored and appreciated. It elevated the whole field."

CHAPTER ELEVEN

Public Education as a Means for Cultural Change

Next to doing the right thing,
the most important thing is
to let people know
you are doing the right thing."

— JOHN D. ROCKEFELLER

THE PUBLIC RELATIONS SOCIETY of America defines public relations as "a strategic communication process that builds mutually beneficial relationships between organizations and their publics." It goes on to state that, "Public relations helps our complex, pluralistic society to reach decisions and function more effectively by contributing to mutual understanding among groups and institutions."

Public relations campaigns typically contain these four steps:

✳ Defining the main objective

✳ Determining the target audience

✳ Crafting the key messages

✳ Developing the plan for reaching the target audience.

Early in its existence, Bravewell recognized the importance of public opinion to the acceptance and growth of integrative medicine. Consumer demand was already exerting some influence in persuading healthcare systems across the country to offer integrative services. But the question was, could Bravewell achieve the main objective—increasing that demand—without spending tens of millions of dollars on a massive public relations campaign?

Bravewell member Bill Sarnoff, who had previously served as chairman of Warner Books in New York, suggested that the Public

Broadcasting System (PBS) might be a strategic venue for presenting the integrative medicine message. PBS was viewed regularly by more than 80% of American households, and health was a significant category in their programming.

Noting that the Bill Moyers series *Healing and the Mind* developed important credibility and forward movement for the field of mind-body medicine, Bravewell members embraced the strategy to create a high-quality PBS series that would tell the integrative medicine story. The sentiment was that if people truly understood what integrative medicine was and how it could help them live healthy, more fulfilling lives, they would demand it of the healthcare system. Thus, with key messages already in place, Bravewell had clarified its main objective and identified its target audience. All that was left was the plan.

DUE DILIGENCE

One of Bravewell's core business practices was that due diligence would always be completed before any work was begun or any strategic decisions made. "Bravewell consisted of many highly successful people," explains Diane Neimann. "Given their background and experience, their expectations were very high. The members were expert investors accustomed to conducting due diligence on any investment they made, and they wisely applied those same standards to philanthropy."

Knowing what was expected of her as the executive director, Diane sought counsel from Judith Moyers, the executive producer for most all of Bill Moyers' work. Judith agreed to advise the Collaborative on a pro bono basis. She told Bravewell, "If you get the best producer that's known to PBS, then you'll stand a better chance of getting it on the air. And if you have a producing station that is among their station networks you'll have a better chance of getting it past the green light committee." She advised that the producing station should be New York, Boston, or Minneapolis.

Essentially, Judith introduced Bravewell to the process of creating a PBS documentary that would air on a national, not just a local, level. "She explained that only ten percent of the shows produced ever aired on national television. That gives you an idea of how high we had to climb," Diane adds.

Securing a highly regarded producer and director was the first hurdle. Early in 2004, the Collaborative's Public Education Committee completed its due diligence, and Middlemarch Films, an experienced and highly respected producer of documentary programming for public television, was retained. Middlemarch had just received an Emmy Award for its production on Benjamin Franklin, which had aired on PBS.

Diane then presented the proposed project to the management team at Twin Cities Public Television (TPT). Highly regarded in the industry for its national productions, TPT had received more than 300 awards, including 25 regional and national Emmy Awards, two Peabody Awards, and an Academy Award nomination. The TPT leadership liked the mission, and once they understood that Middlemarch Films was involved, they agreed to become the sponsoring station.

THE NEW MEDICINE

By leveraging its network of associates, Bravewell raised a total of $4 million in funding for the project. WebMD Corporation and WebMD Health Foundation provided $1.2 million, with Wyeth and Novartis joining the list of corporate donors. Individual members within The Bravewell Collaborative provided most of the remaining funding.

The New Medicine series was completed in early 2006. Episode I, which looked at how science is proving the mind-body connection, featured advances in immunology, neurobiology, and the underlying biological mechanisms involved in healing. The relationships between stress and the immune system and between the brain and treatment of chronic pain were also explored.

Episode II examined the growing acceptance of holistic, mind-body medicine and how it was changing healthcare in areas such as physician training, the hospital environment, and the doctor-patient relationship, ultimately making medicine more humanistic.

Performing due diligence and seeking (and then following) expert advice paid off. The two-part series aired back-to-back on PBS on March 29, 2006 during prime time in all 50 states on 516 stations. More than 4.2 million people watched the first broadcast. Since the initial showing, many PBS stations aired the program again, and total viewership over the initial three-year period reached eight million.

In November 2006, the production was awarded a FREDDIE for excellence in health and wellness media, the nation's highest honor for medical media. The series also won the 2007 Silver World Medal in the Health and Medical Issues category at the New York Film Festival and was nominated for both a News and Documentary Emmy Award and the Peabody Award.

Clearly, *The New Medicine* became a compelling ambassador to the public for integrative medicine.

CHAPTER TWELVE

Friends Across
the Pond

~

"When we seek connection,
we restore the world to wholeness.
Our seemingly separate lives become meaningful
as we discover how truly necessary
we are to each other."

— MARGARET WHEATLEY

B Y 2006, HAVING STAGED two Leadership Award Events, provided funding for the Academic Consortium, the Clinical Network, and the Bravewell Fellowship program, and produced *The New Medicine*, The Bravewell Collaborative was becoming a nationally recognized philanthropic organization known for its innovative and influential accomplishments. While the Collaborative never sought publicity for itself, it nonetheless had become a household name in the world of integrative medicine. As one public relations executive remarked, "That's what happens when you are caught in the act of doing something good."

As the members deliberated about how they might continue pursuing their goal of putting integrative medicine on the national healthcare agenda, the value of developing select strategic partners to leverage the work became apparent.

As always, due diligence played a key role. "The most important thing for me in terms of developing new strategies or protecting the existing strategies was credibility, because integrative medicine's chief problem was credibility," notes Diane Neimann. "So if something or someone might be detrimental to our credibility, that wasn't going to get us where we needed to go. On the other hand, anything that would increase our credibility was something we needed to do.

So when we looked at the people, places, and resources required for change, we always put the question of credibility first."

Part and parcel to this effort were the other criteria used in seeking partnerships: a shared vision, a commitment to scientific rigor, a work ethic built on similar values, and a respected track record in supporting the development of integrative medicine in order to positively affect public health.

By this time, Bravewell had already successfully collaborated with the Academic Consortium for Integrative Medicine & Health, the Center for Integrative Medicine at the University of Arizona, and each of the centers in the Clinical Network. It had also established a partnership with the Arnold P. Gold Foundation to make integrative medicine training more widely available to medical students, and in collaboration with the Robert Wood Johnson Foundation (RWJF), it had co-produced the RWJF Human Capital Clinical Issues Symposium in December 2006, which addressed the effectiveness of integrative medicine for RWJF Fellows and Scholars.

In the coming years, Bravewell would add three more important relationships: HRH Prince Charles' Foundation for Integrated Health, the Institute of Medicine at the National Academies (see Chapter Thirteen), and the Department of Defense and the Veterans Health Administration (see Chapter Fifteen).

THE PRINCE'S FOUNDATION FOR INTEGRATED HEALTH

Long an advocate for integrative medicine, HRH The Prince of Wales created the Foundation for Integrated Medicine (FIH) in Great Britain in 1993 to "promote greater collaboration between conventional and complementary health." (Its name was later changed to the Foundation for Integrated Health.) In 2006, curious about how the FIH was approaching its mission, Diane phoned Kim Lavely, the

Foundation's chief executive officer. "My call to them was simply fact finding," explains Diane. "Could we learn anything? And were there any synergies?"

That and subsequent calls resulted in a deepening relationship. Bravewell members made several visits to the United Kingdom during which they met Mark Leishman, then–assistant private secretary to The Prince of Wales, and Simon Fielding, DO, special adviser on complementary medicine to the United Kingdom's Department of Health. But they were not able to meet with The Prince of Wales.

Once again, however, kismet came to the rescue. In the spring of 2007, John Mack, then-CEO of Morgan Stanley, conducted a Whole Person Leadership Retreat for his management team at Duke Integrative Medicine in Durham, North Carolina. Christy agreed to accompany her husband and entertain the team's significant others by engaging them in a weekend Whole Person Health Program. One of the spouses, Mrs. Lucy Chenevix-Trench, was completely taken by the program and all that was happening at Duke Integrative Medicine. "She told me I needed to meet The Prince of Wales," recounts Christy.

Christy explained how she and Diane had been trying to arrange a meeting for more than a year. "Well, let me see what I can do," Lucy told Christy. And then she unexpectedly added, "My father is Prince Harry's godfather."

Christy already had a trip to London to see her daughter in the planning, so she gave Lucy the dates. "I was packing, and about an hour before I was scheduled to leave the phone rang. It was Lucy Chenevix-Trench."

Lucy told Christy, "You are on. He will meet with you tomorrow."

Christy was astounded. The next day in London, Christy met with The Prince of Wales, Kim Lavely, and Simon Fielding at Clarence House.

After this visit, HRH The Prince of Wales made a commitment

to film a congratulatory video for the upcoming 2007 Bravewell Pioneers of Integrative Medicine Awards Event. Kim Lavely attended the event and a subsequent Bravewell meeting in New York City. Diane and Christy then attended FIH's December 2007 board meeting in the United Kingdom where they presented the work of Bravewell. The two organizations clearly shared a common vision.

LIKE-MINDED ALLIES

Much like the Bravewell Leadership Awards, FIH hosted an awards ceremony each year. In a speech given by HRH The Prince of Wales at the fifth annual Integrated Health Awards Ceremony at the British Academy of Film and Television Arts in Piccadilly, Central London, HRH stated that, "Over the past fifty years we have witnessed the concerted fragmentation of every aspect of our lives and of Nature herself. I happen to believe, for what it's worth, that there is an ever more urgent need for re-integration and for the restoration of harmony and balance. In health and medical terms, this is why I believe so strongly in integrated healthcare—treating the whole person (mind, body, and spirit) with the best of the ancient and modern within medical practice."

A historic "Joint Resolution of Collaboration" was signed between the two organizations on February 25, 2008. FIH leadership also agreed to participate in the upcoming Institute of Medicine Summit on Integrative Medicine and the Health of the Public. Two leading figures in healthcare in the UK—Dame Carol Black, MD, then-chairman of the Academy of Medical Royal Colleges, and Sir Cyril Chantler, FRCP, FMedSci, previous chairman of the King's fund—participated in the Summit Planning Committee and spoke at the Summit. (See Chapter Thirteen.)

From 2008 to 2010, members of The Bravewell Collaborative continued the relationship, which included the funding of two Bravewell

Fellows from the United Kingdom, an act that "has had a lasting legacy," according to Simon Fielding.

"It was an enormous privilege to work with such an extraordinary group of committed, visionary, and competent people who really cared about the need for quality healthcare delivery and knew they could make a difference," adds Simon. "I made some wonderful friends who I will hold in my heart for eternity."

THE SIX LEVELS OF GIVING

In March 2009, Diane, Christy, and Mark Leishman, who had since been promoted to private secretary to The Prince of Wales, presented at the Campden Conference in London, the leading philanthropic conference in Europe and the United Kingdom. Their presentation focused on Diane's prior work concerning the art of collaborative philanthropy and her work with Christy about the six levels of giving, and how Bravewell embodied these principles.

The six levels of giving are:

✳ Donor
  You have decided that giving is an important part of your way of life. You review your most recent charitable activities for trends and interests to document.

✳ Organizer
  You become less reactive and begin to create your own agenda. You make fewer and more-focused gifts.

✳ Evaluator
  You research your highest priority interests, become more strategic, seek new information, retain professional counsel, and confirm the appropriateness of philanthropic vehicles.

✳ Philanthropist
  You maximize your giving, seek solutions, utilize best resources and practices, and measure results.

✳ Collaborator
You leverage your giving, and seek systemic and sustainable change. You find meaning in your work with others. You make a difference.

✳ Leader
You align your values and interests with all of your philanthropic interests. You collaborate and enjoy your success with others. You lead in real social change.

PHILANTHROPY FOR SOCIAL CHANGE

At the November 2010 annual meeting, Simon Fielding reported that due to internal problems, FIH was closing and transitioning its efforts to the College of Medicine. Although the partnership with Bravewell did not continue after FIH closed, the relationships that were built proved to be invaluable.

"We learned from each other," adds Christy. "And because of that, others learned from us."

Philanthropy has always held the power to be the engine for social change. "Philanthropic strategies, fully developed at the most sophisticated level by committed leaders, can be the passing gear for society," remarks Diane. "It can educate the public, move a field, and affect a paradigm shift."

This was always Bravewell's intent.

CHAPTER THIRTEEN

Making Integrative Medicine Part of the National Conversation

❧

"The first step toward change
is awareness."

— NATHANIEL BRANDEN

As Bravewell experienced success and thus confidence, its members continued exploring avenues through which integrative medicine might become part of the national conversation on health and healthcare. While integrative medicine was gaining recognition in certain academic circles and being covered by the popular press, it was not yet part of the ongoing conversation in places like the Department of Health and Human Resources, in the boardrooms of major hospital systems, at insurance companies, or on Capitol Hill.

"As Bravewell, we had purposely stayed away from trying to directly change policy or the insurance industry," explains Christy Mack. "We didn't have the clout, we didn't have the money, and we didn't have the desire to become lobbyists or an advocacy group. So we looked for other leverage points within the healthcare landscape."

"We determined that our efforts to change policy would be best accomplished through education, scientific evidence, and changed perceptions," adds Diane Neimann.

In pursuit of these goals, and at the recommendation of advisors Kathleen Foley, MD, and Ralph Snyderman, MD, Bravewell undertook serious consideration of partnering with Institute of Medicine (IOM) at the National Academies of Science, Engineering and Medicine.

COMING TO AN AGREEMENT

By chance, Christy Mack met IOM's then-president, Harvey Fineberg, MD, PhD, at a dinner function in New York City in September 2007. She introduced him to Bravewell's vision and began to explore the potential for a relationship between Bravewell and the IOM. Dr. Fineberg was receptive, and in October 2007, Christy and Diane met with Ellen Urbanski and Clyde Behney, MD, at the IOM offices in Washington, DC, to outline the partnership and agree on a process, budget, venue, agenda, and plan for a national summit.

During the many discussions with Bravewell, Judy Salerno, MD, MS, the IOM's then-executive officer, came to realize that Bravewell was not talking about complementary and alternative modalities, but rather a *philosophical foundation for care*. "I recognized that Bravewell's message about integrative medicine was totally aligned with the things we cared about," she says. "Health systems are not going to produce good health outcomes until they start including the patient in decision-making. So, for me, the Summit was an opportunity for the IOM to bring those issues to the forefront and to have integrative medicine be understood as something that was necessary to make patient-centered care a reality in this country."

In March 2008, an agreement was signed between The Bravewell Collaborative and the IOM to hold the National Summit on Integrative Medicine and the Health of the Public in the auditorium at the National Academy of Sciences building in Washington, DC, February 25–27, 2009.

IOM senior scholar Michael McGinnis, MD, MPP, was appointed to oversee the project, and IOM member and Bravewell honoree Ralph Snyderman, MD, was chosen to chair the Planning Committee.

"Thanks to our connection with The Prince's Foundation, two distinguished physicians from the United Kingdom—Dame Carol Black of the Academy of Medical Royal Colleges and Sir

Cyril Chantler of the King's Fund—accepted appointments to the Planning Committee," adds Diane. "Having them participate placed the Summit in an international light. Public health is a concern for all nations."

HAVING THE RIGHT AUDIENCE

Bravewell understood that while having the right speakers was imperative (an activity that was within the purview of the IOM Planning Committee and over which Bravewell had no control), equally important was having the right audience. In order for the Summit to make a true difference, the right participants had to be in attendance.

Bravewell members and staff spent the next year identifying leaders who would be in a position to continue the dialogue, take action, and make integrative medicine part of the national agenda following the IOM Summit. Among those organizations invited to the Summit were AARP, American Hospital Association, Robert Wood Johnson Foundation, National Business Group on Health, National Coalition for Cancer Survivorship, National Health Policy Forum, and US Chamber of Commerce.

In addition, Bravewell retained GYMR, a Washington firm that specializes in social change, to coordinate with the IOM to maximize media opportunities and work with me (Bonnie Horrigan) at the Bravewell office to ensure effective public outreach.

THE SUMMIT

The Summit on Integrative Medicine and the Health of the Public, the largest event of its kind ever convened by the IOM, was held February 25–27, 2009 in Washington, DC. It brought together 600 distinguished researchers, practitioners, and leaders from multiple sectors to present the vision, challenges, evidence base, and opportunities for integrative medicine to improve healthcare in the United States.

In his opening address, Harvey Fineberg, MD, PhD, stated that integrative medicine "offered the possibility to fulfill the long-standing World Health Organization's definition of health as being more than simply the absence of disease."

"Harvey made an important point," explains Penny George. "Integrative medicine is built on the recognition that health is a state of physical, mental, emotional, and spiritual *well-being* that enables engagement with life."

In his keynote, Donald Berwick, MD, former president and CEO of the Institute for Healthcare Improvement, spoke about integrative medicine "helping the individual focus on what they 'really, really, really' want."

"For him personally, this meant restoring his physical capacity to cross-country ski to a secluded glade where a certain species of bird sang," Penny recalls. "Integrative medicine, at its heart, is not about therapies at all but about connecting one's health to one's deepest desires."

During the Summit presentations, there was broad recognition that although medical advances have saved and improved the lives of millions, much of our nation's healthcare resources are focused on addressing the effects of specific incidents of disease and injury, while neglecting health promotion and prevention as well as the treatment of underlying mental, emotional, social, and environmental factors that have a significant influence on a person's health.

In offering integrative medicine as a practical model that could help solve many of our current healthcare challenges, Summit faculty urged that "the first priority for a health care system that uses an integrative approach is … to ensure that the full spectrum of prevention opportunities—clinical, behavioral, social, spiritual and environmental—are included in the care delivery process." They further advised that care "should account for the differences in individual conditions, needs and circumstances, and engage the patient as a partner in addressing all the factors that shape wellness, illness and restoration of health."

Important points articulated by Summit faculty were:

✳ Care should be patient-centered

✳ The progression of many chronic diseases can be reversed and sometimes even completely healed by making lifestyle modifications

✳ Genetics is not destiny, and gene expression can be turned on or off by nutritional choices, levels of social support, stress reduction activities such as meditation, and exercise

✳ Our physical and social environment influences our health— the environment outside one's body rapidly becomes the environment inside the body

✳ Improving our primary care and chronic disease care systems is paramount

✳ The reimbursement system must be changed to encourage healthcare providers to focus on the health outcomes of their patients, instead of procedures

✳ Changes in education for healthcare providers will fuel changes in practice

✳ Evidence-based medicine is the only acceptable standard.

Adding to the potential for broad healthcare transformation, Judy Salerno told Bravewell members that IOM recommendations for the Health and Human Services (HHS) reorganization aligned with the Summit, and that it was IOM's intention to broadly share the ideas expressed at the Summit to transform healthcare.

SUMMIT FACULTY AND PLANNING COMMITTEE

*Denotes Planning Committee Member

Nancy E. Adler, PhD, *University of California, San Francisco*

Donald Berwick, MD, MPP, *Institute for Healthcare Improvement*

Dame Carol Black, DBE, MD, FRCP, FMedSci, *Academy of Medical Royal Colleges**

Josephine Briggs, MD, *National Center for Complementary and Alternative Medicine*

Sir Cyril Chantler, *The King's Fund**

Richard Cooper, MD, *University of Pennsylvania*

Thomas Donohue, *US Chamber of Commerce*

Harvey V. Fineberg, MD, PhD, *Institute of Medicine*

Tracy Gaudet, MD, *Duke University*

Mitchell L. Gaynor, MD, *Weill-Cornell Medical Center*

William (Bill) George, *Harvard University*

Elizabeth A. Goldblatt, PhD, *Academic Consortium for Complementary and Alternative Health Care**

Lawrence W. Green, DrPH, *University of California, San Francisco*

Erminia Guarneri, MD, *Scripps Center for Integrative Medicine**

George Halvorson, *Kaiser Permanente*

Senator Tom Harkin, *US Senate*

Michael M.E. Johns, MD, *Emory University**

Janet Kahn, PhD, *University of Vermont*

David L. Katz, MD, PhD, *Yale University*

Mary Jo Kreitzer, RN, PhD, *University of Minnesota*

Richard P. Lifton, MD, PhD, *Yale University School of Medicine**

Mike Magee, MD, *Center for Aging Services Technologies*

Victoria Maizes, MD, *University of Arizona*

Bruce S. McEwen, PhD, *The Rockefeller University**

Arnold Milstein, MD, PhD, *Mercer*

William D. Novelli, *AARP*

Dean Ornish, MD, *Preventive Medicine Research Institute**

Mehmet Oz, MD, *New York–Presbyterian Hospital, Columbia University*

Kenneth R. Pelletier, PhD, *University of Arizona and University of California*

Adam Perlman, MD, MPH, *University of Medicine & Dentistry of New Jersey*

Victor S. Sierpina, MD, *University of Texas Medical Branch**

Ralph Snyderman, MD, *Duke University (Chair)**

Esther M. Sternberg, MD, *National Institute of Mental Health**

Ellen L. Stovall, *National Coalition for Cancer Survivorship**

Kenneth Thorpe, PhD, *Emory University*

Reed Tuckson, MD, *UnitedHealth Group**

Sean Tunis, MD, MSc, *Center for Medical Technology Policy**

Edward Wagner, MD, MPH, *MacColl Institute for Health Care Innovation*

CELEBRATING THE SUMMIT

In November 2009, nearly 300 guests joined The Bravewell Collaborative and representatives from the Institute of Medicine and The Prince's Foundation for Integrated Health for a special event in Washington, DC, to celebrate the official release of the *Summary of the Summit on Integrative Medicine and the Health of the Public*. In attendance were representatives from government, healthcare, education, advocacy groups, philanthropy, and major corporations as well as private citizens. The audience enjoyed a special videotaped speech by HRH The Prince of Wales, Prince Charles.

"This is the way it should be," commented Mehmet Oz, MD, who served as the Master of Ceremonies. "It's going to take all of us work-ing together to transform healthcare and create a culture of health and well-being in America."

POST-SUMMIT OUTREACH

Following the release of the *Summary of the Summit on Integrative Medicine and the Health of the Public*, Bravewell directed its resources to continuing the outreach campaign designed to educate and inspire others to action. Accompanied by Judy Salerno and using the Summit as an entrance point, Christy and Diane spent the next year meeting with policy makers and business leaders in Washington, DC.

"We felt our role could best be played by educating as many people on the Hill as we could about integrative medicine, the work that was being done across the country and the research that was being gathered with regard to its cost, clinical effectiveness, and health benefits," explains Christy.

The enormous effort this required did not escape Judy Salerno's notice. "I admire the folks who came together to start Bravewell," she explains. "They have the resources to spend the rest of their days on a yacht, but these people chose to make a difference in a way that was not just writing a check, but instead, getting in there and rolling up their sleeves and advocating in order to create a movement that would have a strong impact on individuals and eventually on the healthcare system."

"The Summit was a pinnacle for Bravewell," remarks Ann Lovell. "It catapulted the conversation onto the national level, which is what we had hoped for."

CHAPTER FOURTEEN

Building Communities

"Life is systems-seeking;
there is the need to be in relationship,
to be connected to others."

—MARGARET WHEATLEY

IN THE BOOK, *The Community of the Future*, Margaret Wheatley tells us that, "Life takes form as individuals immediately reach out to create systems of relationships. These individuals and systems arise from two seemingly conflicting forces: the absolute need for individual freedom, and the unequivocal need for relationships."

Wheatley goes on to point out that finding balance between these two opposing forces is imperative to building sustainable, thriving communities. She suggests that when we experience problems, we, in community, should answer these questions:

"What called us together?"

"What did we believe was possible together
that was not possible alone?"

"What did we hope to bring forth
by linking with others?"

The leadership of Bravewell instinctively understood these principles, putting their emphasis on the shared vision and values from the very start, while using processes that would enable each person in the group to be heard and feel valued.

They realized that building and protecting a sense of community among the philanthropists was critical to success. "Without a strong sense of community and without creating safe spaces where people could discuss the issues and the work without fear of being judged, we could not have moved forward in the way that we did," explains Diane Neimann.

OPENNESS AND TRUST

That sense of community was one of the attributes that attracted Barry and Janet Lang to the Collaborative. Their introduction to Bravewell began over dinner with Lu and Ann Lovell in 2007. "Lu gave us a copy of the documentary, *The New Medicine*, which was about the power of the mind. That really hit home for me," says Janet. That led the couple to attend a Bravewell meeting to find out more.

"I'm extremely private and typically don't say anything about myself," Barry explains. "Of course, Charles Terry began the meeting by inviting everyone to talk about what was going on in their lives. We started going around the room, and one of the guests confessed that their spouse had just left. At first I thought it was a joke, but it wasn't a joke, and the open honesty floored me."

When his turn came, Barry, who had been planning to say his name and that he lived in Tucson—end of story—shocked himself by saying that he'd been working with a psychologist for a number of years. "I'm trying to retire," he told the group, "and I can't seem to do it."

The whole idea of being in a group of people who shared a common interest and purpose, and with whom it was safe to talk honestly, intrigued both Barry and Janet. After learning about the extent of Bravewell's work during the next day and a half, the Langs became members of The Bravewell Collaborative.

COMMUNITY BUILDING PROCESSES

Bravewell always used a facilitator for their meetings. "The decision to use a facilitator was made early on," explains Diane Neimann, "because it provided a sense of neutrality, and allowed for better participation by members, senior staff, and guest content experts."

Bravewell also included community-building activities in every meeting it held.

"Before the start of the business aspects of the meetings, we engaged in activities that got people out of their everyday roles and everyday selves and into a more creative, more right-brain, and more humanly connected place. We wanted them to leave behind their preconceptions," notes Charles Terry, who facilitated the Bravewell meetings from 2002 to 2015. "You can have all the left-brain skill and knowledge and money there is, but if you don't have this other quality, the deeper human connection, then the outcomes will be different. The work gets done much more effectively when the creative part of our being is engaged."

Some of the processes were simple, such as reading poetry or a favorite quote, starting with meditative silence, or singing a song together. Other activities required more introspection, such as the sharing of recent personal experiences or telling the group something about oneself that the group did not know. Being in the group as people, rather than job titles or social positions, shifted the atmosphere and in some cases, broke down barriers.

In Lu Lovell's opinion, "The sharing was impressive. People shared what was in their hearts and what was going on in their lives. I trusted that whatever I said would not be belittled or dismissed, that it would be considered as part of an intelligent dialog. I trusted people to keep my confidences. In any community, trust and honesty are huge."

BRAVEWELL IS FAMILY

Blythe Brenden's grandfather had been sick for many years before he died. In an effort to make him as comfortable as possible, Blythe's family, the Minneapolis-based Manns, arranged for acupuncture treatments and massage therapy, among other things. The interventions were helpful. "I know it helped prolong his life," Blythe explains. "It made the remainder of his life so much better."

Later, when Bill and Penny George were seeking donors to help support the Penny George Institute for Health and Healing at Abbot Northwestern Hospital in Minneapolis, they contacted the Mann family. Blythe's mother volunteered Blythe to co-chair the initial capital campaign, which is how she got to know the Georges.

In 2007, Penny and Bill invited Blythe to come to the Leadership Award Event in New York and then attend the Bravewell meeting the next day. She said yes, but not with the intention of joining Bravewell. For her, it was simply an opportunity to learn more about integrative medicine. But the meeting completely changed her mind.

"There was something about sitting in a room full of people who had the same mission, the same vision, the same passion, and the same commitment," Blythe explains. "It's about friendships and about relationships. We were not being judged. All of our voices were heard. I am on a lot of boards, and it is not like that in other places. This was a group that worked together and was bonded by something that was much bigger than themselves. For me, Bravewell is family."

PROTECTING THE COMMUNITY

"We all realized from the get-go that *protecting our sense of community, and the creation of safe spaces*, was critical," explains Christy. "That meant, however, that we had to make some tough choices."

"In the beginning we thought the more members we could recruit, the better it would be," notes Ann Lovell. "But we soon learned that bigger was not necessarily better and that not everyone was suited to Bravewell's philosophy and operating principles. But staying lean was a hard decision because it meant less money from other people."

"Staying lean" wasn't easy on numerous levels. Sometimes, when it was obvious the fit wasn't right, people left on their own accord, and sometimes they were encouraged to move on.

"Many very wealthy people have made their mark by not collaborating, but instead, by just doing what they want to do," explains Bill Sarnoff. "Some of those people stayed for a few years and then moved on, and that is okay."

"We recognized from the outset that we were asking a great deal of people when we reached out to them to become members: that because of the significant commitment of personal time and resources required, this would be their primary philanthropic involvement," Penny adds. "So we were clear that people could come and go over time, and we were grateful for their sharing any part of the journey with us."

Still, on occasion, feelings ran high. "I wish there had been a manual that explained how to part ways in a manner that did not hurt people's feelings," says Christy. "But there wasn't such a book, so we did the best we could. Having said that, I would never take our actions back. I think those tough conversations and hard decisions helped to cement and set the precedent for people's reasoning for coming to Bravewell. I think it helped us to make wiser decisions about recruiting future members."

This strong sense of community, and the fact that a core group of the membership joined and stayed, contributed to the programmatic success Bravewell was able to achieve because there was continuity. "Longevity of commitment is important," explains Bill George. "With many organizations, there is a constant rotation of players. But with Bravewell, we had the consistency of that long-term vision and commitment. The same players are still around. The founders—my wife Penny, Christy Mack, Bill Sarnoff, and Ann and Lu Lovell—stayed from the start to the finish. Likewise, on the medical side, many of the same players are still involved and still engaged—people like Brian Berman, Mimi Guarneri, Dean Ornish, and Andy Weil."

CONNECTION AND PASSION

Michele Mittelman's introduction to integrative medicine started in nursing school, where she was trained to view patients holistically and to understand that each person's health or disease state was a function of many interrelated and complex effects within the body, mind, and spirit. "I appreciated the high-tech medical advances that were making great strides in curing patients, but my greatest satisfaction was the difference I could make working one-on-one with a patient to help them understand and manage the range of emotional and physical experiences they were encountering," explains Michele.

Later, when her young daughter fell seriously ill with continuous ear and respiratory infections, conventional medicine was not able to help. Her daughter kept relapsing. Searching for answers outside of the mainstream, a homeopathic doctor prescribed the remedy *natrum sulphuricum*. It worked. And that propelled Michele on a journey to find out more about integrative medicine.

Although they weren't acquainted, Michele and Penny George owned vacation homes near one another in the Colorado Rockies, where they spent time each summer. When Penny and Michele finally did meet, and Michele heard about Bravewell, she was intrigued. After attending a Bravewell meeting, Michele knew she was in the right place.

"The most important thing for me was that everyone was working as a group toward a common goal," explains Michele. "The members shared connection and passion. It was a collective, collaborative effort, and I loved that."

STAYING ON COURSE

Protecting the community also involved keeping Bravewell on track. "One of the toughest things for me was to remind the philanthropists that we couldn't go charging off after every new idea," explains Diane.

The discipline of picking the right strategies and then staying with them—and not being pulled off track by the next great idea—was a staff imperative. "It's not that we didn't make adjustments when we had to because we did, but when you are trying to do something as big as effect social change you have to stay on course," Diane adds.

NOT EVERYTHING WORKED

It is important to note that not every potential partnership Bravewell pursued resulted in actionable items, and that some ideas, pursued eagerly, were also abandoned just as eagerly.

"Some of the things we tried simply didn't ripen," explains Penny. "But that was okay. When that happened, we knew enough to let go, regroup, and move on."

A LEARNING ORGANIZATION

Another activity Bravewell used to build community was to stage an educational session before their meetings. For instance, at one meeting an executive from the consulting firm IDEO led the group through a visioning process. At other times, Sharon Reis from GYMR presented on how to run a successful educational campaign; Martin Seligman, PhD, professor at the University of Pennsylvania, gave a presentation on positive psychology; and Robert Sapolsky, PhD, professor at Stanford, talked about stress.

Bravewell was a continuous learning organization and because of those sessions, the members collectively grew together.

THE HIGH ROAD

It is also important to acknowledge that, of course, not everything was perfect. Far from it. As with any group of human beings trying to accomplish something together, over the years there were disagreements, disappointments, tensions, and hurt feelings. As many Bravewell members understood, "That's just human nature." But one of the most impressive aspects of Bravewell was how often the philanthropists, and to some extent the staff, chose the high road. They chose not to "sweat the small stuff" as the saying goes, but to keep their eye on the ball instead. Often, not only could they set aside their own agendas, but also their own frustrations, to keep the larger vision alive.

"By and large, the philanthropists were highly curious and not afraid to learn from their mistakes," explains Diane. "In that sense, I would say that Bravewell was a forgiving organization."

BRAVEWELL MEMBERS

Members at the time of closing:

Blythe Brenden, *The Brenden-Mann Foundation: 2008–2015*

Penny George, *The George Family Foundation: 2002–2015*

William (Bill) George, *The George Family Foundation: 2002–2015*

Barry Lang, *Philanthropist: 2008–2015*

Janet Lang, *Philanthropist: 2008–2015*

Ann Lovell, *The David C. and Lura M. Lovell Foundation: 2002–2015*

Lu Lovell, *The David C. and Lura M. Lovell Foundation: 2002–2015* (deceased)

Sherry Lund, *Philanthropist: 2003–2015*

Christy Mack, *The Christy and John Mack Foundation: 2002–2015*

Michele Mittelman, *Michele and David Mittelman Family Foundation: 2005–2015*

William (Bill) Sarnoff, *Philanthropist: 2002–2015*

Former Members:

Diana Andrus, *Philanthropist: 2006–2008*

John Baillie, *Philanthropist: 2004–2005*

Ruth Baillie, *Philanthropist: 2004–2005*

Earl Bakken, *The Earl and Doris Bakken Foundation: 2002–2007*

Ira Brind, *Philanthropist: 2002–2007*

Myrna Brind, *Philanthropist: 2002–2007*

Georgine Busch, *The Earl and Doris Bakken Foundation: 2002–2007*

Bruce B. Dayton, *Philanthropist: 2002–2007*

Fiona Druckenmiller, *Philanthropist: 2005–2007*

Mark Finser, *Rudolf Steiner Foundation: 2004–2006*

Barbara Forster, *Philanthropist: 2005–2010*

Richard Fox, *Philanthropist: 2003–2005*

Lynn Getz, *The Globe Foundation: 2002–2007*

Jane Hein, *Philanthropist: 2006–2007*

Joanne Heyman, *The Karan Weiss Foundation: 2008–2011*

Virginia Hubbell, *Mental Insight Foundation: 2003–2008*

Colby Jones, *Philanthropist: 2003–2011*

Lani Jones, *Philanthropist: 2003–2011*

Donna Karan, *Karan-Weiss Foundation: 2006–2011*

Ron Mannix, *The Norlien Foundation: 2002–2006*

Nancy McCabe, *The Kohlberg Foundation: 2002–2006*

Ron Simms, *Philanthropist: 2004–2006*

Vicki Simms, *Philanthropist: 2004–2006*

Linda Stone, *Philanthropist: 2004–2006*

Ruth Stricker, *Philanthropist: 2002–2007*

David Surrenda, *Fannie E. Rippel Foundation: 2005–2008*

Ruth Westreich, *The Westreich Foundation: 2007–2012*

A COMMUNITY OF ADVISORS

"Another thing I think we did well from the beginning was to form connections with all kinds of thought leaders and to build relationships with them," explains Diane. "I always felt that I could pick up the phone and get good advice. For instance, behind the scenes, the Moyers advised us on who to hire for the PBS Special, who was good, who was not, and that made all the difference in the world."

Bravewell used its networks. Through Diane, Christy, and Penny, Bravewell had access to philanthropic circles. Through John Mack and Bill George, it had access to business leaders. Through the Moyers and Bill Sarnoff, it had access to people in communications and the media. And through physicians such as Ralph Snyderman and Kathy Foley, Bravewell had access to academic medicine and to public institutions such as the IOM and NIH.

BRAVEWELL ADVISORS

Georgine Busch, *The Earl and Doris Bakken Foundation*
Simon Fielding, DO, *Prince's Foundation for Integrated Health*
Kathleen Foley, MD, *Memorial Sloan-Kettering Cancer Center*
John Mack, *Morgan Stanley*
Judith Moyers, *Public Affairs Television, Inc.*
Diane Neimann, *Family Philanthropy Advisors, Inc.*
Mehmet Oz, MD, *The Dr. Oz Show*
Father Walter Smith, *The Healthcare Chaplaincy*
Ralph Snyderman, MD, *Duke University Health System*
Ellen Stovall, *National Coalition for Cancer Survivorship*

"We were all well connected," explains Bill Sarnoff. "That's a very important point when looking at the history of Bravewell. It couldn't have happened without all the connections."

"We should be forever grateful to all of these people," Christy adds.

STAFF

"Having the right staff is key to any philanthropic success," explains Bill Sarnoff. "We were lucky in that our staff was very helpful in keeping us on track." And then he adds, as so many others have echoed, "I think Diane, our founding executive director, was a brilliant strategist and visionary."

As the founding executive director, Diane Neimann set the bar high for staff performance. "If I felt responsibility for anything it was to give the philanthropists value for their investment," she explains. "The strategies had to be good but the philanthropists also had to get what they needed out of them, and for each individual that was something different. So I felt that part of my role, which often was difficult, was to help everyone find out where they could make a contribution and to also ensure that whatever we did, we did really well so that they could see that their philanthropy had been effective."

As anyone in philanthropy knows, often money is given, but the desired outcome is never achieved. "I think being able to see progress toward their goal kept the most committed of the philanthropists in the group," Diane adds. "Bravewell's ability to execute, to bring good people into the work, and to maintain the highest of standards was a critical strategy. If the goals had never been achieved, the group would not have stayed together. So you could say that we understood that, in order to make all the other strategies work, one of our top priorities was that the organization perform at a high level."

In 2011, I (Bonnie Horrigan) assumed the role of executive director, succeeding Diane Neimann, who had retired. "We originally hired Bonnie as our communications director as she is one of the few writers/journalists who had been with the field since its beginning in the early 1990s, and consequently has true depth of knowledge," explains Diane. "Her skills and expertise soon made her integral to many of Bravewell's initiatives and finally, to the role as executive director."

Another key employee was Ellen George, Bravewell's chief operating officer. She was the organizing mind behind the Leadership Award Events and was instrumental in keeping the office on track both organizationally and financially.

"Clearly a large part of Bravewell's success was the efficiency and effectiveness of the administration," says Charles Terry. "The philanthropists provided the vision and the money, and the staff kept it grounded. The fact that there was a strong collaboration between the staff and the philanthropists contributed to making the organization run smoothly. Each side played a significant role. I've done a lot of work in philanthropy, and having such a collaborative relationship between the philanthropists and the staff is very unusual."

KEY STAFF

Diane Neimann, *Founding Executive Director (2002–2008)*

Bonnie Horrigan, *Executive Director (2011–2015); Director of Communications and Public Education (2005–2010)*

Ellen George, *Chief Operating Officer (2002–2013)*

Jeneen Hartley Sago, *Program Officer (2007–2012)*

Benjamin Kligler, MD, MPH, *Medical Advisor (2011–2015)*

Constance Pechura, PhD, *Scientific Advisor, (2007–2012)*

Charles Terry, *Philanthropic Advisor and Facilitator (2002–2015)*

CHAPTER FIFTEEN

Unexpected Allies

"When you walk to the edge
 of all the light you have
 and take that first step
 into the darkness of the unknown,
 you must believe that one of two things will happen.
 There will be something solid for you to stand upon
 or you will be taught to fly."

— PATRICK OVERTON

leadership—Christy Mack and Penny George—to attend a meeting at the Pentagon.

Among those present from the Department of Defense (DoD) were Brig. Gen. (Dr.) Richard Thomas, Assistant Surgeon General, Force Projection; Col. Kevin Galloway, Chief of Staff, Pain Management Task Force; Dr. Kathy Quinkert, Special Assistant to Vice Chief of Staff; and Col. (Dr.) Patricia Lillis-Hearne, Walter Reed Army Medical Center.

Key information presented at this exploratory meeting included:

✳ Huge numbers of armed services personnel were dealing with chronic pain

✳ Most treatment was by way of over-the-counter and prescription medication, especially opioids

✳ Soldier suicides, accidental overdoses, medication abuse, and substance abuse were all major problems

✳ Many soldiers were already utilizing complementary modalities at their own initiative and expense

✳ The Army believed its culture of care needed to radically change

✳ The Army wanted to partner with people with experience

✳ The Army was willing to implement integrative medicine protocols that were supported by research outcomes, while at the same time engaging in new research to learn more.

Following the initial meeting, representatives from The Bravewell Collaborative and the PMTF participated in several meetings, the goal of which was to explore a collaborative partnership that would assist the Army in developing and implementing a standardized approach to pain management.

As the ability to work with a large, single payer such as the Armed Forces represented a phenomenal opportunity, a small working group was appointed to move the collaboration forward. The team consisted of Donald Abrams, MD; Tracy Gaudet, MD; Mimi Guarneri, MD; Bonnie Horrigan; Christy Mack; and Connie Pechura, PhD. Diane Neimann, who had retired, reprised her role as Bravewell's advisor to help develop the strategies for collaboration.

Bravewell drafted a proposal, "The Way Ahead," and presented it to the PMTF. The idea for a "command briefing" was suggested as a means to engage key Army decision-makers, provide a clear case for the implementation of the PMTF recommendations, and build credibility for the program and its leadership such that all DoD decision-makers would embrace the program and fully support it within their spheres of responsibility. After reviewing the proposal and engaging in further conversations, the Army embraced the idea of the briefing.

Integrative Medicine—The Way Forward: Army Comprehensive Pain Management Campaign Plan Symposium was held on June 23, 2011 at the Pentagon. Army Surgeon General Eric Schoomaker gave the opening remarks, followed by a presentation by Lt. General David Fridovich, recently retired head of Special Operations. The Fridovich speech was especially compelling as it chronicled his personal struggle with chronic pain and the difference that integrative medicine approaches had made for him. Bravewell arranged the morning's sessions, which included presentations from Kathy Foley, MD; Mimi Guarneri, MD; a panel from the Allina Health System (Kenneth Paulus; Penny Wheeler, MD; and Lori Knutson, RN, BSN); and retired Brigadier General Steve Smith, Chief Human Resources Officer for the Duke Health System. The afternoon featured a panel of military and VA researchers and clinicians including Wayne Jonas, MD, from the Samueli Institute, and Rollin (Mac) Gallagher, MD, and Tracy Gaudet, MD, from the VA.

SHARING RESEARCH

In late March 2012, Col. Galloway requested that Bravewell propose a small group to begin to formally advise and collaborate with the DoD and VHA to develop and implement a standard set of patient outcomes measures across DoD, VHA, and private sector sites. The ongoing dialogue focused on aligning changes to the Patient-Reported Outcomes Measurement Information System (PROMIS) to make the data collection process more streamlined and clinically useful, and the creation of an alliance of research institutions who would utilize PROMIS with the intent to compare data from different clinical settings.

Col. Galloway introduced the Executive Committee of BraveNet, Bravewell's practice-based research network, to Col. Chester Buckenmaier III, the lead researcher for the Army's pain initiative and its Pain Assessment Outcome Registry (PASTOR) effort, which was the army's program that collected patient-reported outcomes using the PROMIS measures. At this same time, Bravewell had a similar research program that used the PROMIS measures that was named PRIMIER (Patients Receiving Integrative Medicine Interventions Effectiveness Registry). Ongoing meetings with Col. Buckenmaier and his staff focused on how to make PASTOR and PRIMIER as compatible as possible, so that the combined databases could provide a resource for researchers studying integrative approaches to care. (See Chapter Sixteen.)

THE VETERANS HEALTH ADMINISTRATION (VA)

During the IOM Summit, Tracy Gaudet, MD, then–executive director of Duke Integrative Medicine, developed a relationship with a general from the VA who was very interested in her speech and the rest of the Summit content. As a consequence, in the following year, VA leadership—who like the Army was very interested in better pain management and improving the patient care experience—traveled to Duke to see what was being done within its healthcare system.

In 2010, the VA created the Office of Patient Centered Care and Cultural Transformation with the mission of transforming the VA's health system from a traditional medical model that was focused on treating specific issues to a personalized, proactive, patient-driven model that promoted whole health for veterans and their families. Tracy was ultimately recruited away from Duke to be the VA's Director of Patient-Centered Care and Cultural Transformation.

"I was hired to ensure that the VA transformed from physician-centered care to personalized, patient-centered care that is based on relationships, built on trust, and committed to positive results over the veteran's lifetime," explains Tracy. It was a daunting task. "That goal represented one of the most massive changes in the philosophy and process for healthcare delivery ever undertaken by an organized healthcare system," she adds.

Bravewell reached out to Tracy and, as with the DoD, began the work of establishing a collaboration for outcome data collection with the VA. In May 2013 the BraveNet Executive Committee met with Tracy and her team, including a number of senior VA researchers, in Washington, DC, to discuss potential collaboration using the PRIMIER model.

In June 2014, Ben Kligler, MD, MPH; Bonnie Horrigan; and Christy Mack met with Tracy Gaudet, MD; Barbara Bokhour, PhD; Rani Elwy, PhD; Kenneth Mizrach, MD; and others at the New Jersey VA to specifically discuss the New Jersey VA's involvement in PRIMIER. Soon thereafter, the New Jersey VA decided to pursue formal participation.

Barbara Bokhour, PhD, director of the Bedford Center for Evaluating Patient Centered Care in the VA, and Rani Elwy, PhD, health psychologist and health services researcher with the VA, attended the fall meeting of BraveNet. Drs. Bokhour and Elwy have since deployed a feasibility study of the PRIMIER protocol at the VA clinics in East Orange, New Jersey; Los Angeles, California; and Washington, DC.

In addition, Bravewell invited the VA to officially join BraveNet, an invitation the VA readily accepted.

"The sharing of ideas and practices will move this national transformation forward at an even faster pace," Tracy predicts.

CHAPTER SIXTEEN

Proving the Case
for Integrative Healthcare

⁓

*"What we find
changes who we become."*

⁓ PETER MORVILLE

I N 1997, IN TESTIMONY BEFORE the Senate Committee on Labor and Human Relations, Subcommittee of Public Health and Safety, Harold Varmus, MD, then-director of the National Institutes of Health, told Congressional leaders that, "Clinical research has changed the face of modern medicine. Fifty years ago, at the end of World War II, physicians had little ability to effectively treat or prevent any of the deadliest diseases. Most of the staples of modern medicine we enjoy today were still unknown: antibiotics, vaccines for polio and several other severe infections, most hormone replacements and steroid therapy, effective drug therapies for cancer and psychotic illnesses, testing for genetic disorders, coronary bypass surgery, transplanted organs, and artificial joints."

He went on to point out that more recent advances in care for diseases such as cardiovascular disease, diabetes, and cancer would not have happened without an ongoing clinical research effort. "The take-home message is simple," he said. "Every one of these advances and opportunities they engender is dependent on a sustained and heightened clinical research effort."

The case for integrative medicine would be no different. Without clinical research, the field would never advance. While Bravewell had chosen not to fund research in and of itself, the 2003 McKinsey Report advised the Collaborative to develop a practice-based research network (PBRN) that would help advance integrative medicine by providing clinical use, clinical outcomes, and cost-benefit data.

As Brian Berman. MD, explains, "A PBRN is a group of medical practices principally devoted to the primary care of patients that have affiliated with each other in order to investigate questions related to clinical practice. The main component of such a network is an online, computer-based infrastructure that allows for the collection, tabulation, and sharing of data among clinicians not in the same location."

INTEGRATIVE MEDICINE RESEARCH

Most conventional research measures the effect of a single intervention or biologic agent against another single intervention, but, as practiced, integrative medicine utilizes a multitude of interventions, so that all the factors contributing to the state of a person's mind, body, and spirit are addressed. For instance, conventionally, one might compare a pharmaceutical dosage to an acupuncture session. But acupuncture given as a stand-alone treatment is rarely what happens in an integrative clinic. To get an accurate picture of integrative medicine's effectiveness, one should compare a pharmaceutical for pain with, for example, a regime of acupuncture, meditation, massage, and changes in diet. Hence, the real power of a PBRN is not only its ability to study the effectiveness of specific interventions, but to also examine the benefits of a true integrative approach to care.

The funding of the infrastructure for this network, aptly named BraveNet, was an activity Bravewell could embrace.

"The idea behind creating a PBRN for integrative medicine was to bring a group of clinicians and practices together in order to answer questions and speed up the application of research findings into everyday clinical practice," explains Brian Berman, MD, director of the Center for Integrative Medicine at the University of Maryland, who spearheaded the initial effort. "In essence, it's the clinical laboratory for collecting important patient-centered data and a way to engage clinicians in the research process."

The leadership for the PBRN was eventually transitioned to the Duke Clinical Research Institute (DCRI) at Duke University. In 2009, under the direction of Rowena Dolor, MD, MHA, director, Primary Care Research Consortium at DCRI, BraveNet completed a Registry Study, which examined the demographics of the patients presenting at the integrative medicine clinics. A second effort, Study of Integrative Medicine Treatment Approaches to Chronic Pain (SIMTAP), examined integrative medicine outcomes for patients with chronic pain. SIMTAP results showed significant reductions in pain and improvements in mood and quality of life for patients treated with an integrative approach.

BraveNet SITES AS OF JUNE 2015

✳ Alliance Institute for Integrative Medicine, *Cincinnati, Ohio*

✳ Program for Integrative Medicine at Boston Medical Center, Boston University, *Boston, Massachusetts*

✳ Center for Integrative Medicine at the University of Colorado Hospital, *Denver, Colorado*

✳ Mount Sinai Beth Israel Center for Health and Healing, *New York, New York*

✳ Duke Integrative Medicine, Duke University, *Durham, North Carolina*

✳ Jefferson–Myrna Brind Center of Integrative Medicine, Jefferson University, *Philadelphia, Pennsylvania*

✳ Center for Integrative Medicine, University of Maryland, *Baltimore, Maryland*

✳ Osher Center for Integrative Medicine at Northwestern University, *Chicago, Illinois*

✳ Osher Center for Integrative Medicine, University of California, San Francisco, *San Francisco, California*

✳ Center for Integrative Medicine at University of Pittsburgh Medical Center, *Pittsburgh, Pennsylvania*

✳ Penny George Institute for Health and Healing at Abbott Northwestern Hospital, *Minneapolis, Minnesota*

✳ Scripps Center for Integrative Medicine, Scripps Health, *La Jolla, California*

✳ Simms/Mann Health and Wellness Center at the Venice Family Clinic, *Los Angeles, California*

✳ Osher Center for Integrative Health at Vanderbilt University, *Nashville, Tennessee*

PRIMIER

In 2012, Jeffery Dusek, PhD, research director for the Penny George Institute for Health and Healing at Abbott Northwestern Hospital, conceived of a BraveNet project that would combine patient reported outcomes with data from the patient's electronic medical records into a large dataset that could be used for quality improvement, evidence-based research, and determination of "best practices." Called PRIMIER, the objectives were:

❋   To evaluate the change in patient-reported outcomes (e.g., quality of life, mood, stress, etc.) over time

❋   To evaluate whether patient-reported outcomes differ by baseline characteristics of the participants (e.g., demographics, clinical condition, interventions used).

Through the collection of patient-reported outcomes on a number of frequently seen medical conditions, and by clustering the patients from multiple integrative medicine sites into subsets with the same medical condition, researchers are then able to compare the impact of various integrative therapies. This approach allows researchers to gather evidence on a much larger scale than would be possible in a typical clinical trial at a single institution. With more than 2000 patients enrolled in PRIMER to date, this unique data registry is already providing foundational new knowledge on how integrative medicine is being used in real-world settings and offering an early glimpse into where, with the use of integrative medicine, improvements are being seen.

   When asked his opinion about the potential for PRIMIER to make a difference, in a 2013 email to Christy Mack and Bonnie Horrigan, Bravewell advisor Ralph Snyderman, MD, said, "I think this is a *good* idea and a *big* idea."

   Bravewell members embraced PRIMIER and funded the project

as part of their final legacy gifts to the nation. As mentioned in Chapter Fifteen, BraveNet has now begun to partner with DoD and VA researchers to create comparable databases.

INTO THE FUTURE

Knowing that Bravewell would be sunsetting and that the DCRI could no longer provide coordinating center services after 2014, a search committee consisting of Bonnie Horrigan; Donald Abrams, MD; and Jeffery Dusek, PhD, was charged with finding a new home for BraveNet and PRIMIER. In the summer of 2014, on the committee's recommendation, Bravewell members unanimously chose Albert Einstein College of Medicine as the new coordinating center for BraveNet, with leadership being provided by Einstein's Co-Director of Research, Diane McKee, MD, MS, and Benjamin Kligler, MD, MPH, the new BraveNet chair.

"PRIMIER represents an unprecedented opportunity to evaluate the outcomes of integrative healthcare. Its strengths lie in the diversity of patients, practice settings, clinicians and services reflected in the registry, which will facilitate a wide range of analyses," says Diane McKee. "Because PRIMIER data is drawn from real world practice, findings about what works will have immediate relevancy to clinicians and patients."

At its closing, noting the importance of this work, Bravewell made an additional grant to Einstein to carry BraveNet and PRIMIER forward into the future.

CHAPTER SEVENTEEN

A New Type of Leader

❧

*"The greatest leader is not necessarily
the one who does the greatest things.
He is the one that gets the people
to do the greatest things."*

— RONALD REAGAN

AS PART OF THE SUNSETTING PROCESS, Bravewell members deliberated on what they could do in the way of a final legacy gift that would advance the field of integrative medicine well beyond the time when Bravewell closed its doors. This important conversation went on for more than a year.

"We didn't want to just write a final check to someone and walk away. We wanted to use our remaining funds in such a manner that the whole field would benefit," explains Penny George.

After they informed the clinical network members of their plans to sunset—an announcement that was met by a profound silence—Bravewell members asked the physicians what final project might move the field forward. Several ideas were put forth, but one that kept surfacing was that *the field needed leaders*. Possessing the very best clinical skills would not help people in leadership positions understand how to overcome organizational resistance. It wouldn't help them to write a business plan that the C-suite would get excited about, nor would those clinical skills help them build the type of relationships they would need to transform the culture of healthcare.

While the members liked the idea of creating a program that would teach leadership in the context of integrative medicine, no one knew if the concept "had legs." With due diligence called for, they established a committee consisting of Michele Mittelman, Bonnie Horrigan, and Ben Kligler and charged them with researching the need for, and the potential viability of, such a program.

In June 2012 in San Francisco, under the committee's direction, a think tank comprised of key integrative medicine leaders brainstormed the concept, discussed program content and structure, and suggested possible ways to move the initiative forward.

LEADERSHIP THINK TANK MEMBERS

✳ Maureen Arkle, MPH, *Marino Center for Integrative Health*

✳ Kevin Barrows, MD, *UCSF Osher Center for Integrative Medicine*

✳ Rocky Crocker, MD, *University of Arizona Center for Integrative Medicine*

✳ Bonnie Horrigan, *The Bravewell Collaborative*

✳ Benjamin Kligler, MD, MPH, *Mount Sinai Beth Israel Center for Integrative Medicine*

✳ Lori Knutson, RN, BSN, *Allina Health Systems*

✳ Victoria Maizes, MD, *University of Arizona Center for Integrative Medicine*

✳ Michele Mittelman, *The Bravewell Collaborative*

✳ Adam Perlman, MD, MPH, *Duke Integrative Medicine*

✳ Kieran Richardson, MA, *University of Arizona Center for Integrative Medicine*

✳ Bill Stewart, MD, *California Pacific Medical Center*

The think tank determined that the program's goal should be *to cata-lyze the transformation of American healthcare* by training leaders to incorporate integrative care into hospitals, academic health systems, public health clinics, community hospitals, and private practices, thus improving the quality of care, lowering costs and increasing patient participation and satisfaction. Four primary content areas were identified as being crucial: (1) transformational leadership, (2) integrative health and the healthcare environment, (3) prevention and well-being, (4) communication and business operations.

With a program description that could be shared, the committee then engaged in formal market research through GYMR, Bravewell's ongoing public relations firm, and held lengthy discussions with Joe Denucci, former general manager of Miraval, and other business leaders within the field. Upon determining that no such course already existed and that the need was real, Bravewell moved forward with a Request for Proposal (RFP) process.

Bravewell told potential RFP respondents that, "We need health-care leaders who understand the immense value of conventional medicine as well as the promise of integrative care and who can create collaborative environments in which the best of both can be realized."

A formal grant agreement to create such a program was signed in July 2013 with Duke Integrative Medicine/Duke University.

Conceived in collaboration with Duke's Fuqua School of Business, the program structure was designed as a one-year experience that included a combination of in-person leadership immersions, online course work, and a mentorship during which the students would write a business plan to be implemented at their institutions.

WHAT IS INTEGRATIVE LEADERSHIP?

"Part of the program creation process was to examine how, if one stayed true to the principles of integrative medicine, an integrative leader might differ from more conventionally trained executives," explains Adam Perlman, MD, MPH, who serves as the leadership program director in addition to his other duties at Duke.

A small team consisting of Adam Perlman, MD, MPH; Bonnie Horrigan; Elizabeth Goldblatt, PhD; Victoria Maizes, MD; and Benjamin Kligler, MD, MPH, brainstormed that question and, in 2014, collectively wrote *The Pebble in the Pond: How Integrative Leadership Can Bring About Transformation.*

During this process, the development of mindfulness emerged as a foundational value. Widely embraced within integrative medicine, mindfulness refers to a particular way to deepen self-awareness and increase one's ability to stay present in the moment. Founder of the Center for Mindfulness in Medicine, Health Care and Society at the University of Massachusetts Medical School, Jon Kabat-Zinn, PhD, explains that mindfulness is awareness that is "cultivated by *paying attention* in a sustained and particular way: on purpose, in the present moment, non-judgmentally."

Under Adam Perlman's direction, faculty added the act of being properly "informed" to the concept of mindfulness. "Informed mindfulness connects mindful self-awareness and self-regulation with educated decision-making," explains Adam. The mindful person is aware, non-judgmentally, of what is occurring in the present moment and understands that his or her response is a choice. But what are those choices and which one is best? The course emphasizes continued learning so that when situations arise and decision points are faced, people are not only able to place what is happening in its larger context but, having clear values and being sufficiently educated, they are able to make an *informed choice* within that moment.

"The only place you can make change is in the present, so we teach mindfulness to patients to help them heal, and we teach mindfulness to our co-workers to help them thrive," adds Lori Knutson, RN, BSN.

The program's core faculty advocate that good leadership begins from within and is based on:

* The continued deepening of mindful awareness

* The development of values—especially integrity, authenticity, compassion, courage, humility, and passion

* A commitment to increasing knowledge, skills, and wisdom in self and others.

THE LEADERSHIP PROGRAM IN INTEGRATIVE HEALTHCARE AT DUKE

Within a year and a half of Duke's receiving the Bravewell grant, the first cohort enrolled in the Leadership Program in Integrative Healthcare at Duke University. A second cohort began their program in February 2016.

"I think this program is critically important and one of the most potent initiatives that will affect a real transformation of healthcare," explains Michele Mittelman. "Clinicians don't necessarily have the leadership skills to bring about change. But when you bring a like-minded group together to learn those leadership skills, and they have time to interact with each other, it helps to cultivate their passion. And as they share, it reveals the path."

"This program is training the future leaders of healthcare," adds Christy Mack.

FACULTY
LEADERSHIP PROGRAM IN INTEGRATIVE
HEALTHCARE AT DUKE UNIVERSITY

*Denotes Core Faculty

John Anderson, MD, MPH, *Duke University*

Michael C. Aquilino, *Innovational Services**

Michelle Bailey, MD, *Duke University*

Dan Baker, PhD, *Consultant*

Douglas Borg, MA, *Duke University*

Sanjiv Chopra, MD, *Harvard University*

Michael Cohen, JD, MBA, MFA, *Consultant*

Bridget Duffy, MD, *Vocera Communications Inc.*

David Eisenberg, MD, *Harvard School of Public Health*

James Emery, PhD, MBA, *Duke University*

Tracy Gaudet, MD, *Veterans Health Administration*

Elizabeth Goldblatt, PhD, MPA/HA, *Academic Consortium for Complementary and Alternative Health Care*

Thomas Bolt Gosselin, MA, *Consultant and Executive Coach*

Aviad Haramati, PhD, *Georgetown University*

Sanne Henninger, PhD, *Duke University*

Bonnie Horrigan, *The Bravewell Collaborative**

Janet Kahn, PhD, *University of Vermont*

Karen Kingsolver, PhD, *Duke University*

Benjamin Kligler, MD, MPH, *Mount Sinai Beth Israel and Albert Einstein College of Medicine**

Lori Knutson, RN, BSN, *Meridian Health**

Kaihan Krippendorff, MBA, *Outthinker*

E. Allan Lind, PhD, MA, *Duke University*

Annie Nedrow, MD, MPH, *Integrative Physician*

Adam Perlman, MD, MPH, *Duke University**

Kevin Pho, MD, *KevinMD.com*

Marcia Prenguber, ND, *Oncologist*

Scott Reeves, PhD, MSc, *Kingston University/St George's, University of London*

Sharon Reis, MA, *GYMR*

Jennifer Rose, MBA, *Duke University*

Sim Sitkin, PhD, EdM, *Duke University*

Linda Smith, PA-C, MS, *Duke University*

Stephen Smith, MAE, *Duke University*

William Sollecito, DrPH, *UNC Gillings School of Global Public Health*

Myles Spar, MD, MPH, *Venice Family Clinic*

Dwan Thomas-Flowers, MBA, *Consultant*

David Victorson, PhD, *Northwestern University*

Kory Ward-Cook, PhD, MT, *National Certification Commission for Acupuncture and Oriental Medicine*

Claudia Witt, MD, MBA, *University of Zurich*

Shelley Wroth, MD, *Duke University*

CHAPTER EIGHTEEN

Saying Adieu

~ᴟ~

"Endings are not bad things;
they just mean that something else
is about to begin."

— C. JᴏʏBᴇʟʟ C.

B RAVEWELL FORMED IN 2002 with the intention that one day it would no longer exist.

"I think one of the smartest things we did was to put a timeline to our efforts," explains Christy Mack. "We knew we didn't want a never-ending story. None of us wanted that. So we gave ourselves ten to fifteen years to change how Americans thought about their health and the kind of healthcare they received, and to bring about the cultural change necessary to create a healthier nation."

"The decision to have a firm beginning and ending kept us focused," adds Christy. "We all knew time was of the essence. It also kept us from taking on additional projects that we did not have either the money or the time to take on."

True to this sentiment, when their principal strategies were completed and integrative medicine was finally part of the national conversation on healthcare, Bravewell members took note and collectively decided that the time was right to sunset the organization.

"Our mission was to try to quicken the pace of bringing integrative medicine into our healthcare system, make people aware of it, and make it part of everyday life," adds Bill Sarnoff. "We helped that along. There can be discussions about how much or how little, but clearly we did have some effect."

WITH GRATITUDE FOR ALL INVOLVED
"Integrative medicine is now part of mainstream culture and that is

largely due, not only to Bravewell, but to all those involved," says Penny George. "This includes the clinicians, the university professors, the researchers, the authors, the healthcare and hospital executives, the patients, and the media—everyone who championed the cause."

"We will be forever grateful," adds Christy Mack. "Together, we made huge strides in making prevention, patient empowerment, and healthy living part of the nation's priorities. And together we developed the core template for care that addresses not just the body, but also the patient's mind and spirit."

Bravewell closed its doors in June 2015.

In contemplating Bravewell's absence, Christy adds, "Progress will continue. The ranks have swelled, and now thousands of others are carrying the torch forward."

DEMONSTRATING A NEW MODEL OF PHILANTHROPY

In a 2015 letter to Bravewell, Jon Kabat-Zinn, PhD, wrote, "Back in the old days, when I was a student at MIT, I once attended a talk by Jay Forrester, a pioneer of the Sloan School there, who said that he thought institutions should be designed to dissolve in their seventh year, which should be ample time to make the contribution that they set out to make and then dissolve. But to my knowledge, no one has ever done that, in seven years, or in seventy years. So you have pioneered a model that we all could learn from, and in the process, have changed the world of medicine and healthcare, and even more, the mind set and heart set of the field and in no small way, the world."

CHAPTER NINETEEN

Reflections

> "Follow effective action with quiet reflection.
> From the quiet reflection
> will come even more effective action."
>
> — PETER DRUCKER

ZEITGEIST IS A TERM that means the "spirit of the age" or the "spirit of the time," and refers to the school of thought that typifies and influences the culture of a particular period in time in a particular place.

In his book, *What Makes It Great*, Rob Kapilow writes, "There are certain unique moments in history, what one might call 'zeitgeist moments,' when an artist or a group of artists can seem to be almost miraculously in sync with the larger society's needs and interests: moments like the Renaissance in Florence, the flowering of the opera in Italy, the birth of the classical style in Vienna, the second Viennese school at the turn of the twentieth century, Paris in the teens and twenties. The art of these moments can seem to grow almost inevitably out of the spirit and circumstances of the time."

Within the world of healthcare, Bravewell members were among those "artists" who helped give voice to a zeitgeist moment in which a new paradigm for health and healing was illuminated.

THE PERFECT FRIENDLY STORM

It could also be, as Diane Neimann puts it, that, "There was something in the air."

During the 1990s, certain people across the nation started working to transform the healthcare system in a way that would recognize the intelligence of nature, honor the wholeness of the patient, and return the soul to medicine. But they were not doing it together. They were each doing it on their own. Yet they were all part of the same emerging movement.

In reflecting on why integrative medicine has reached a tipping point in its acceptance and use, Michele Mittelman comments that, "The *timing* of several factors converging at the same point was serendipity at its best. Those factors include consumer dissatisfaction with the present state of healthcare, the emergence of anecdotal and scientific evidence that supported the concepts within integrative medicine, the coalition of entities (government, foundations, clinical, research) that stepped forward, and a passionate group of individuals with related personal experiences who believed in the possibility for change."

Ralph Snyderman, MD, agrees. "Often, there is a confluence of forces that, in and of themselves, would not be sufficient to really move the needle, but when they all come together at the same time, sometimes for different reasons, you get that crystallization that makes something much bigger happen," he says.

This is what happened with integrative medicine.

"It was the perfect friendly storm," adds Christy Mack. "I don't believe there's a day that goes by that Bravewell isn't grateful for what it has been fortunate enough to experience, because somehow things aligned and we came together at the right time. There was a true synergism of passion, wealth, wisdom, work, connections, and collaboration."

A GESTALT

In talking about how Bravewell advanced the field and in trying to make sense of what emerged, some people used the word "gestalt," which refers to a theory that an organized whole has an independent existence and will be different than the sum of its parts. The whole becomes something in and of itself.

Herb Stevenson of the Cleveland Consulting Group states, "A gestalt changes perceptions and therefore what people believe is possible by supporting awareness to emerge from the existing ground of possibilities and potential. Reality shifts by widening, deepening, and revealing new or alternative ways of thinking, perceiving, and therefore doing."

In a significant way, Bravewell contributed to the formation of an integrative medicine gestalt.

A THOUSAND LIGHTS

Bill George says that what happened with Bravewell was similar to the metaphor President George H. W. Bush used in his acceptance speech at the 1988 Republican Convention. President Bush compared America's clubs and volunteer organizations to "a brilliant diversity spread like stars, like a thousand points of light in a broad and peaceful sky."

"We let the thousand lights shine," Bill says. "We brought them together into a big glowing star in the sky. That is the way I see it. The lights shone. And we uncovered all kinds of lights that shone that we didn't even know were there."

Adding to this, Ann Lovell notes that, "When you have an intention and you open up fully to all the possibilities, things happen that you could have never predicted."

KEY FACTORS AT WORK

Bravewell elevated the integrative medicine movement. It helped the concept become a "gestalt" that was and is alive in our culture, and it illuminated the zeitgeist of the time. And while its members were certainly moved by the "spirit of the times," you cannot ignore the intelligence, forethought, and love of life with which they acted. As many people noted during the interviews for this book, "Fourteen other people could have gotten together, and nothing would have happened."

"We weren't the founders of the field," remarks Penny George. "But we arrived at the right time with philanthropic help. And in a certain respect, that gave the field of integrative medicine increased credibility, which in turn had its own ripple effects."

Hard work was also in the equation. "Part of our success came from taking the steps that would make a difference no matter what those steps took. We were willing to commit our money, our hearts, and our time to the vision," adds Ann Lovell.

Having the right resources was a significant factor. "We were very fortunate in having substantial philanthropists involved," explains Bill Sarnoff. "Money was never a difficult problem. We could do most everything that we had a vision to do, and I think that's reasonably unique."

Equally important was having the right attitude. "We had respect for one another and acted in accordance," he adds.

In reflecting on Bravewell's 14 years of existence and addressing the creation of an effective philanthropic organization, Christy offers this advice: "Maintain your integrity above all. Speak honestly and directly. Whatever you do, do it with passion. Do it with intelligence and wisdom. Do it in collaboration. Motivate each other. Stay friends. Safeguard your community of collaborators. Vet your partners well. Take on that larger vision—it's large because it's so important. Shoot for the moon. Go for the gold. Ask for heaven, and start at the top. If you do all that, you'll be happy with where you land."

PRINCIPLES FOR ORGANIZATIONAL SUCCESS

In its early years, Bravewell identified the following principles as being critical to its vision and mission and then used them to inform their decision-making, build their relationships, and guide their work.

✳ Collaborate
Working together, a group can accomplish more than any one individual could accomplish alone.

✳ Maintain a Shared Vision
It is vital to have each member of the group hold the same vision and define success in the same way.

✳ Remain Dedicated to the Mission
Staying focused is crucial to success. Don't get distracted or go off target.

✳ Agree on Key Values and Principles
Values drive personal behaviors. Well-defined operating principles drive organizational behaviors.

✳ Define Clear and Achievable Goals
It is crucial to have well-defined goals that can be accomplished by the group and/or its partners and which are not dependent on forces beyond the group's control.

✳ Leave Self-Interest Behind
Every individual in a collaborative has his or her own agenda. But for the work of the collaborative to succeed, self-interests must be left behind and the best interests of the shared work must be paramount.

✳ Engage in Sustainable Activities
Good financial management of the collective resources and the design of projects that fit within budgets is a must.

✳ Find the Leverage Points
Conducting good research and analysis is key to choosing the right initiatives—initiatives that are far-reaching and result in systems change. Act strategically.

✳ Grow a Community
Attention to deepening the bonds between members of the group pays off in spades.

✳ Manage by Consensus
As much as possible, include everyone in the decision-making process.

✳ Use Tough Love
Knowing when to say no to a proposed initiative, or when to gracefully walk away from a relationship, may be hard, but it is a skill worth having.

✳ Find the Right Partners
Knowing how to vet and choose partners is crucial. Don't compromise long-term viability for a donation of any amount or what appears to be an easy fix to a problem.

✳ Don't Reinvent the Wheel
If something is being done well by others, don't duplicate it. Partner with them.

✳ Create Synergy
When possible, and if it fits the mission and vision, help advance what is already in process of emerging.

✳ Support Innovation
The human capacity to be creative is what underlies our continual evolution.

✳ Engage in Continual Self/Group Education
Never stop learning.

✳ Create Change as an Insider
Partner with the system you want to change.

✳ Hire Competent Staff
The competence of staff can make or break an organization.

✳ Utilize a Good Facilitator
A non-biased facilitator can help the group deliberate and evolve.

✳ Build Mutual Respect and Trust
Respect is the foundation for success.

PHILANTHROPY AT ITS BEST

Bravewell's role in changing how Americans think about health and medicine is an example of what philanthropy is capable of accomplishing at its very best.

"For me, the Bravewell years were transformative," explains Penny George. "My journey began with my body, my physical self. But by working on a shared vision with deeply committed fellow travelers from within both medicine and philanthropy, I experienced emotional and intellectual, and even spiritual, growth beyond anything I could have imagined."

"Bravewell practiced the true definition of philanthropy, which is 'affection for mankind,' the love and caring expressed in doing good for others," adds Christy Mack. "There is no greater calling than to live in service of others, no matter what form that service takes."

ACKNOWLEDGMENTS

I WORKED FOR THE BRAVEWELL COLLABORATIVE from 2005 until its closing in June 2015 the last four years of which I served as the executive director. It was, undoubtedly, one of the most exciting and satisfying times in my life. As I told Christy Mack one day, "Best job, best people, best outcomes—ever." When we knew that sunsetting was imminent, I encouraged the Bravewell members to engage in a project that would preserve the history of their endeavor, because I felt their work was too important to simply let it fade into the vastness of things gone by. At the time, I was thinking more in terms of creating a library of their papers. But the result of those conversations became this book. They asked me if I would write it, and it was a challenge I readily accepted. By the way, if you think you felt love within these pages, you did.

BONNIE HORRIGAN

I would like to thank the following people for helping to make this book possible:

Harvey Fineberg, MD, PhD, president of the Moore Foundation, for writing the eloquent foreword.

Christy Mack, Penny George, and Diane Neimann for being mentors extraordinaire.

Marilyn Petterson, Sheldon Lewis, and Margaret Chesney for being "readers" and offering their astute editorial advice.

Sheldon Lewis for copyediting the book and saving me from the embarrassment of misplaced commas and misspelled words.

Anne Kerns of Anne Likes Red, Inc., for creating the beautiful book design.

Sharon Reis and Tamara Moore at GYMR for their expert assistance in marketing and public relations for the book.

Laura Degnon of Degnon & Associates for stepping up to the plate and agreeing to oversee the whole project.

The leadership of the Academic Consortium for Integrative Medicine & Health for assuming the role of the book's publisher.

BIBLIOGRAPHY

Wheatley, Margaret, and Deborah Frieze. "Using emergence to take social innovation to scale." *The Berkana Institute* 9, 2006.

Lave, Jean, and Etienne Wenger. *Situated learning: Legitimate peripheral participation.* Cambridge University Press, 1991.

Horrigan, Bonnie, Sheldon Lewis, Donald I. Abrams, and Constance Pechura. "Integrative medicine in America—how integrative medicine is being practiced in clinical centers across the United States." *Global Advances in Health and Medicine* 1, no. 3 (2012):18–94.

Ancona, Deborah. "Sensemaking: Framing and acting in the Unknown," in *The Handbook for Teaching Leadership: Knowing Doing, and Being.* Snook SA, Nohria NN, Khurana R, Eds. Sage Publications, Inc., 2011.

Prahalad, C.K., and Gary Hamel. "The Core Competence of the Corporation." *Harvard Business Review*, May 1990.

Wheatley, Margaret J., and Myron Kellner-Rogers. "The Promise and Paradox of Community," in *The Community of the Future.* Jossey-Bass, 1998.

Rob Kapilow. *What Makes It Great.* John Wiley & Sons, 2011.